FINDING THE WILL OF GOD
IN A CRAZY MIXED-UP WORLD

Tim LaHaye

FINDING THE WILL OF GOD

IN A CRAZY MIXED-UP WORLD

PYRANEE BOOKS

Zondervan Publishing House
Grand Rapids, Michigan

FINDING THE WILL OF GOD IN A CRAZY, MIXED-UP WORLD
Copyright © 1989 by Tim LaHaye

Pyranee Books are published by
the Zondervan Publishing House
1415 Lake Drive, S.E.
Grand Rapids, Michigan 49506

Library of Congress Cataloging-in-Publication Data

LaHaye, Tim F.
    Finding the will of God in a crazy, mixed-up world / Tim
LaHaye.
        p. cm.
        "Pyranee books."
        Bibliography: p.
        ISBN 0-310-27171-1
        1. Christian life—1960– 2. God—Will. 3. Decision-making
(Ethics) I. Title.
        BV401.2.L31536   1989   88–36538
                                                                    CIP

Printed in the United States of America

89 90 91 92 93 94 / ML / 10 9 8 7 6 5 4 3 2

Contents

1

Eleven People
Who Made
Difficult Decisions

"Life is so complex today! I'm afraid I'll miss the
will of God for my life."

"My life is so mixed up and complicated that I
don't know what to do!"

These are typical cries I've heard through the
years. It seems to be increasingly difficult even for
God's people to make correct decisions—not because
God has changed but because life has radically
changed. This world is infinitely more complex today
than it was just a generation ago, and it will doubtless
become even more so as the high-tech, social, and
spiritual revolutions continue to gather momentum.

The following stories describe some of the people
who've sought my help in finding God's will. They
represent the hundreds of people who come with
complex problems and decisions, needing to find God's
direction for their difficult situations. Although the

names used in these examples are fictitious, the stories themselves are very real. In fact, these stories may remind you of your own situation or that of a relative, friend, or neighbor.

As you read through these examples, ask yourself, "How would I begin to look for God's will in this situation?" You will not find answers to that question in this chapter; my purpose here is to relate only the complex decisions these people faced. Later in the book, however, I will use each of these stories to illustrate biblical techniques that can help you make the difficult decisions that will mold the course of your life.

The Widow with Three Sons

Joan, an attractive, thirty-nine-year-old woman, approached me for counseling, identifying herself as a "widow" with three sons. She told me that she had fallen in love with a Christian man who had two daughters similar in age to her boys. Their mother had died of cancer a little over two years before. "We've been seeing each other for the past year and a half and are very much in love," Joan explained. "We have many things in common, he's a spiritual leader in our church, and all the children enjoy each other. They look forward to having new brothers and sisters."

As she spoke, I thought to myself, *What's your problem? The situation certainly sounds ideal to me.* Then she revealed the difficulty. "My husband, a major in the Air Force, had been a pilot throughout our marriage. But seven years ago he was shot down over Vietnam, and after four years of being listed as missing in action, the government declared him dead. For three years I've carried this knowledge, not knowing for sure if he's alive or dead. What should I do? If I marry Bob, whom I now love, and Charles is found in a prison camp and released, I will have betrayed him, our sons, and our marriage vows. But if Charles really is dead and I refuse to marry Bob, I'll be destroying what happiness we could have together and the normal family life we could give to our children. I've prayed diligently about this matter, but the Lord hasn't given me an answer. What should I do?"

As you know, this bizarre situation is not an isolated case in this crazy, mixed-up world. Joan obviously needed supernatural wisdom. As I'll illustrate later, she received it.

Should the Unfaithful Husband Tell?

A very distraught father of three children who attended our Christian school came in for counseling. With much effort Dick haltingly told his story. This forty-year-old Christian was very successful at two professions, his regular job and the Amway business he'd started just four years earlier. In fact, the Amway business was doing so well that he felt he could soon quit his eight-to-five job to have more time with the family.

Then it came tumbling out. Dick had been unfaithful to his wife. "Only once, I swear it! But it's driving me crazy. I love my wife and am so guilty about what I did that I'm having problems with male impotence for the first time in my life." I wasn't surprised, for I've seen guilt make a virile twenty-five-year-old man impotent.

Dick had met an attractive, outgoing Christian woman at an Amway convention. They had spent too much time together making provision for "the flesh," which the Bible warns us not to do. First they chatted, then they sat together, then they had coffee, soon they ate meals together—and then it happened. It was difficult to tell who propositioned whom, but Dick spent one night in this happily married woman's room.

"We never plan to see or hear from each other again. Both of us have no intention of ruining our marriages and disgracing our families. We just got carried away and are ashamed of what we've done. We want to put this behind us—but I can't. It haunts me whenever I crawl into bed with my wife.

"I've confessed my sin to God, and I never want to let myself get so spiritually low that I do a thing like that again—it just isn't worth it. But what should I do about my wife? If I tell her, I'm afraid it'll kill her—or make her frigid! What do I do?"

By using some of the principles outlined in this book, Dick also discovered God's will for his situation.

The Unwed, Pregnant Teen

Two brokenhearted parents and their obviously pregnant seventeen-year-old daughter came in for counseling. The daughter, Becky, wasn't intentionally loose with her morals. She was a Christian who had even witnessed to many of her friends in school, but during the past few months she'd lost interest in spiritual things. She hadn't gone to church camp the previous summer and had attended church and youth activities only sporadically. Becky felt that sex with her popular, athletic boyfriend was necessary to maintain their relationship and bask in the sunlight of his popularity. Although our youth pastor had tried to intervene early in this relationship, Becky had rejected his attempts.

Now, of course, she was very repentant. "I've ruined my whole life," she cried. Her parents were determined to give Becky loving support as she confronted this difficult trauma. But the situation was further complicated by the fact that the boyfriend—not a Christian—had offered to marry Becky. What should they do? What was God's will in this disastrous situation?

Picking Up the Pieces After Divorce

Fran, a woman who lived with an unrepentant, unfaithful husband, told me her story.

In 1954, I fell in love with a handsome, life-of-the-party non-Christian. When I agreed to go out with him, I had no idea I would end up being his wife. I also was certain I could change him after we married.

What a heartbreak trip I took! But for the grace of God I could be a very bitter, angry person.

In 1961, he went forward to receive Christ at a Billy Graham Crusade. He was very happy for a few years, and we were active in each church we attended. He was transferred frequently by his employer, but we always found a good Bible-believing church.

His job increasingly required him to travel. The more he was away from home, the more his old lifestyle haunted him. He began to frequent bars, and his infidelity returned. He rebelled against the church, no longer studied Scripture, and stopped seeing our Christian friends.

You may wonder why I stayed with him for as long as the marriage lasted. No one I knew ever divorced. No one in our families ever divorced; it wasn't even thought about as an action to take.

In 1983, he left our home, our church, and all our friends. After thirty years of marriage, he divorced me in 1984. Our whole church rocked with the sad news; he was on almost every committee and board and was very active in sports at the church.

What should Fran do? What is God's will for her shattered life? We'll see later how God used godly advisers to reveal His will.

Your Temperament Is Showing

While speaking at a Christian camp, an attractive twenty-seven-year-old counselor surprised me with a most unusual request. "Will you do me a favor?" she asked. "When you speak in my home church next month, will you ask Tom, the youth pastor, either to marry me or get out of my life?" I thought to myself, *What am I getting myself into?* Then she explained that she had been going with the youth pastor for several years and that they'd been engaged eight times. But every time he approached the wedding day, he had broken the engagement—twice after the wedding invitations had been sent out!

Both young people were dedicated Christians. They had attended a four-year Christian college together, after which Tom had spent two years on a mission trip before becoming a successful youth pastor. While Tom professed that he loved his fiancée, he also vacillated in his commitment to her. She was so tired of his vacillation that she finally said, "I either want to marry Tom or never see him again so I can get on with my life."

When I spoke at Tom's church the next month, he came to me at lunch one day and said, "I have a problem." Then he narrated the same story his fiancée had related. "What is God's will for me?" he asked.

This youth pastor's situation was complicated by his temperament. Decision making came hard for him, as it usually does for the capable, analytical Melancholic. My advice to Tom, based both on an understanding of his temperament and on God's principles, helped him make what has turned out to be the right decision. Later in the book we'll see what decision he made.

The High Price of Sin

The following story moved me about as much as any I've ever received—partly because it didn't reflect the attitude of a loose woman. I share Alison's story not only because it's true but also because it illustrates the high price we pay for sin. The Bible declares, "The way of transgressors is hard" (Prov. 13:15b KJV), and this Christian woman would certainly agree.

> I've been a single parent for six-and-a-half years; my son is ten, and my daughter is twelve. Six weeks ago I committed adultery with a very close friend who is separated from his wife. We didn't plan to become sexually involved; it happened in a moment of our weakness. We are both Christians, and I asked forgiveness but was still, of course, filled with guilt.
>
> Well, three weeks ago I confirmed that I was pregnant. For the first time in my entire life, I felt a true sense of hopelessness. So many times in the last six or seven years I've felt that I was handling all I could. How could I possibly do more with my time, finances, emotions, etc.? I lost my job and am only working part-time now. I have no maternity insurance.
>
> In desperation I scheduled an appointment for an abortion at 9:30 on Wednesday morning, know-

ing it was terribly wrong but feeling that having a child under these circumstances was just as wrong. Then my daughter broke her ankle; I had to take her to the doctor and was forced to cancel my appointment. I rescheduled for the next morning, feeling relieved to a degree, for the moment, but cancelled again on Thursday morning and rescheduled for Friday. Finally I realized that I had to stop this cycle. I needed to start to obey God and His Word. I've got to believe that He will guide me and lift me up from my enemies at this time. I still have to tell my children (both Christians) and my friends and family. Please pray for me, my family, and this unborn, special child. We have many decisions ahead of us and need God's guidance.

Alison has found God to be her strength, even in the aftermath of her sin. She experienced God's forgiveness, but that didn't change her pregnancy and all the related consequences. How will she find God's will for the life ahead of her? Later in the book we'll discuss the principles that helped Alison.

I'm Married to a Porno Freak

During the break at one of my Family Life Seminars, a thirty-five-year-old wife asked to see me privately. I learned that sixteen years before, Nancy had married a fine Christian man, who was a good provider. They had three children, and until four years ago they had enjoyed an ideal marriage.

Gradually Nancy noticed her husband was changing, not only finding excuses to skip church but also asking her to be involved in bizarre sexual practices. "I went along with him for a while, not because I liked it but because I wanted to be a submissive wife. I hoped it was only a fad that would soon pass. But it didn't. Gradually his demands intensified, and our love life turned into a gruesome orgy that left me feeling degraded and ashamed before God." Then Nancy described some practices that are too explicit to include in this book—activities that I hear about at almost every seminar as I review the participants' written answers to questions we ask. In Nancy's case, I sensed pornography was part of the problem. When a person's tastes reveal a reprobate mind, I suspect an artificial stimulus; most people don't think such depraved thoughts on their own.

Nancy quickly confirmed my suspicions and said she'd found some pornographic magazines under her mattress. When she had confronted her husband with them, she learned he was addicted to pornography.

What was Nancy to do? What was God's will for her? She asked, "Do I have to submit to my husband's unnatural demands? I can't stand to live like this and have seriously considered divorcing him." I shared a biblical answer with her, identifying options that pointed her to the will of God. We'll explore that answer in another chapter.

The Printer Who Saved $42,000

One day Ron, a young member of my men's discipling class, came to me with a worried look on his face. "I didn't sleep much last night," he began. "I've decided to expand my printing company and have found another printer who has agreed to merge our two companies. He wants to leave the business in five years. With the down payment of $42,000, which I can afford, we'll formulate a five-year partnership. At that point I'll own the whole thing.

"Today we're supposed to sign the papers. At first I had peace about it, but as time went on, I felt uneasy about it. Now I can't even sleep. So after my wife and I had our devotions this morning, she suggested I come over and talk to you about it. What should I do?"

I asked Ron one question, based on a fundamental Bible principle, and the answer saved him $42,000 (less the cost of the dinner for our wives and ourselves, which he paid for in celebration). You, too, can use that principle.

The Minister Who Had an Affair

A minister and his wife came in for advice about the affair John had with one of the female leaders in his church. John and his wife were in their late thirties, had four children, and were enjoying a growing congregation. He was an outstanding preacher but experienced a running battle with ego and lust—and lately he'd been losing.

John claimed his sexual involvement with the other woman was limited to one incident. His wife added that John had confessed the adultery to her, and the other woman also had told her spouse. The two couples then had met together to confess their part in it all and to pray together. All four of the people are trying to forgive each other and rise above it.

"But one question remains," John continued. "Should I leave the church? Or should I hope the truth never comes out and continue serving the Lord where He seems to be blessing?" What is God's will for this pastor? How will God direct him to pick up the pieces of his life?

The Captain Who Wants to Be an Admiral

A close personal friend of mine came to talk about some difficult career decisions he needed to make. Ted may be the first Navy pilot to become a captain at age thirty-four. Able to fly anything the Navy had in its arsenal, he had held almost every important post on his meteoric climb to the top except one—the command of a ship or a base. And he needed one or the other if he ever were to become an admiral. Ted knew that if he didn't get one of these positions soon, he would be passed over.

When we had our talk, Ted faced three choices, all of which would affect his high-school-age children. He could stay where he was as a squadron commander; he could trust God for a command post that would open the door to his future; or he could resign the Navy and accept an offer from a major aircraft firm to become a test pilot. If he did the latter, his income would increase substantially (if he stayed alive), he would work more regular hours, his kids could stay at the Christian high school they liked, and the family could remain in the church they loved.

As I prayed for wisdom, I did what one can do only under very specific circumstances. Remember, I know Ted well. He's very dedicated to God, a man of the Word who seeks God's perfect will in all the major, moderate, and minor decisions of life. Looking him in the eye, I asked, "What do you really want to do?"

Without a moment's hesitation, Ted replied, "I've wanted to be a Navy flier and officer all my life. I'd like to reach for the brass ring." Did Ted have a right to "reach for the stars"? What was God's will for my Navy captain friend? We'll find out in another chapter.

Politicians Need Guidance Too

A friend of mine, a Christian congressman whom I'll call Stan, wanted to become the U.S. senator from his state. That's not uncommon here in Washington. Unfortunately, Stan had attracted lots of competition for the Senate race from his own party, several of whom were as conservative as he. After he had made his official announcement and was busy raising money, he discovered that three local politicians were vying for his seat in Congress.

What was Stan to do? He wanted to serve God in the political arena, but what was the best place for him to do that? The basic question was: How could he find God's will for his future?

Summary

By now you may be saying, "Wait a minute. I'm not a congressperson, military officer, or preacher. I'm just a sinner saved by grace, trying to make the most of my life." That's true of everyone. And the best part of all is that your heavenly Father has a will for your life.

But finding His will is not automatic. You must follow His road map, heed His Spirit's leading, and obey the signs He gives along the way.

▷ *Just remember this: no one ever failed to do the will of God because God didn't reveal His will in time to do it.*

Anyone who fails to identify God's will has had to stumble over His Word, His leading, the advice of friends, and the "coincidences" He occasionally arranges for you, just to get your attention.

The fact that you are reading this book may just be one of those "coincidences."

My Most Traumatic Decision

All the important decisions we make in life are not confined to our youth. I had served the Lord for almost thirty years when I made the most difficult decision of my life. I shudder to think what my life would be today had I strayed from the center of God's will.

I share this story with you early in this book to let you know that I'm not writing about abstract principles. When it comes to finding God's will in a complex age, I've been there. My life-changing decision affected not only my life but also the lives of my wife, my family, and thousands of other people, several hundred of them quite acutely.

After pastoring the same church for twenty-five delightful years, I felt God leading me to resign and enter another area of service. Very honestly, it was the most traumatic decision I've ever made—and it changed my life much more graphically than I had anticipated. I never dreamed it would involve a 3000-mile move from our home in San Diego to a condominium in Washington, D.C. I can honestly say that God answered my simple but earnest prayer: "Lord, please don't let me get out of Your will by making a mistake in this matter. In fact, heavenly Father, if this is really what You want me to do, I beg You to give me such confidence that I'll never second-guess the decision or feel that I made a mistake."

I have only one fear on this earth—that I would ever get out of the will of God. And you probably share that fear—that's why you're reading this book. We all know that happiness and blessing are bound up in doing His will. It's not just that we selfishly want to be blessed; we know that we have only one life, and it must count for God and His kingdom. Getting out of His will obviously prevents us from accomplishing His perfect will for our life.

And that's what I wanted—God's perfect will for my life. But what was that perfect will? Was it to leave the pastorate or to stay? The church I was pastoring at the time had grown in size ten times during that twenty-five-year period. We had started a quality Christian high school that developed into one of the largest Christian school systems in the nation. We began Christian Heritage College, which mothered the Institute for Creation Research, and they helped found Family Life Seminars. In all, the church (one church in three locations) owned almost fifty acres of property valued at close to $16 million, with less than $2.5 million of debt. Our total income for all the entities was close to $10 million annually. Best of all, the Lord had built up a worldwide missionary program so that it could honestly be said, "The sun never sets on the ministry of the Scott Memorial Baptist Church." Thousands of people were touched there each year by the Spirit of God, and I could have been content, had the will of God permitted it, to spend the rest of my life as the pastor of those churches.

During the six years since I left that church, I've at times missed being a pastor. After all, pastoring had been my life for thirty years (including a church in Minneapolis). I've often observed, "You can take the pastor out of the church, but you can't take the church out of the pastor." But I can honestly say God answered my prayer! Never one time have I doubted that God led me to make that difficult decision.

I won't kid you—it hasn't been easy. Some of our dearest friends and loved ones on this earth continue to live in southern California. Two of our sons-in-law are still youth pastors on the staff of that church, and three of our children still live there, along with all eight of our grandchildren. But every day God has given me the assurance that I made the right decision. And that's what I desire for you, particularly when it comes to the major decisions of your life.

And don't misunderstand. Some people suggest that when we take a gigantic step of faith, everything comes up roses. That hasn't been my experience! In fact, I've never had my faith tested more than when I left the pastorate. Yet in times of certain failure and difficulty, God has always supplied my need and extended my ministry. Frankly, I hadn't expected to start a ministry all over again, but for all practical purposes, that's what happened. Only lately have I seen the evidence of God's leading in tangible terms—yet He has never permitted me to doubt that He led me in making one of the most important decisions of my life.

Scripture tells us that God is faithful (1 Cor. 10:13; 2 Tim. 2:13; Heb. 10:23; etc.). I've put Him to the test in my life and found Him so. By the time you finish this book, you, too, will be equipped to make right decisions about finding God's will for your life.

Admittedly, I haven't always obeyed the Lord, and for a time in my early life, I slipped completely out of His will. Fortunately, such periods were short lived, and none of the big decisions were made during that period, so I was spared the frustration of fouling up my life. If you've already short-circuited your life to some extent, don't despair. There's hope for you. Follow the principles outlined in this book and get your life back on track as soon as possible so you don't miss God's perfect will.

I'm certain of one thing: as life in the next decade gets more complex, it will become even more difficult to find the will of God. But it is possible! God has promised, "Then you will call upon me and come and pray to me, and I will listen to you. You will seek me and find me when you seek me with all your heart" (Jer. 29:12–13).

Finding God's Will in a Crazy, Mixed-Up World

Your life today is the net result of your decisions— good or bad. The older you get, the more those decisions influence you. Some choices affect you minimally: what to wear, what to eat, or how to get to work. Other decisions, however, affect your entire life: whom you marry, where you work, whether or not you become a Christian.

Your life is full of decisions—major, moderate, and minor. Major decisions have major consequences; they often chart the course of your life. Moderate decisions seriously influence your life, but they aren't life molding: they may involve deciding whether to have three or four children or deciding whether to live in the city or the suburbs. The minor decisions only slightly affect your life.

You make minor decisions many times a day, but they gain weight when added together. When, for example, people rebel against God and make many minor decisions contrary to His Word, they can create serious difficulties for themselves. Usually bad minor decisions can be rectified quite simply, although they do create unnecessary pain. Of the three types of decisions you make, some occur only once in life; some can be altered (but with great difficulty); and some are frequently made, changed, and repeated. For further clarification examine the categories below.

Major Decisions

Major decisions have a life-directing influence on you. They include:

1. *Salvation.* The most important decision you will make is whether to accept or reject God's offer of salvation and eternal life.

2. *Vocation.* While you can change your vocation, you often lose important time that can't be regained.

3. *Marriage.* Unless death or divorce take your mate from you, this is a once-in-a-lifetime decision.

4. *Education.* If you choose to get education beyond high school, the college, university, or trade school you attend and the friends you make there often influence your life for as long as you live.

5. *Commitment to obedience.* An important major decision is the degree to which you commit yourself to obeying God's will, both His revealed will and His specific plan for your life. And it's a decision you need to reaffirm every day. The key to the Christian life is to

walk in the Spirit every day of your life—a decision that involves surrender to His will (Gal. 5:16–18; Eph. 5:18).

Moderate Decisions

While moderate decisions influence your whole life, they can be altered or remade more easily than major decisions. They include:

1. *Where you work.* Once you have chosen a vocation—like accounting, for example—you choose whether to use that skill in a large company or small, within the insurance field or the food industry, etc. This moderate decision affects your life, but it can be changed two or twenty-two years later.

2. *Where you live.* Deciding whether to live in a condominium or a house, whether to live in Michigan or Florida are moderate decisions. They can be changed five or fifteen years later with only moderate consequences.

3. *Where you go to church.* Deciding whether to join a small Baptist church or a large Methodist church or a neighborhood house church is a moderate decision.

4. *Your friends.* Choosing a circle of friends is a moderate decision. Friends influence our lives, but they also can move away or change interests and leave our circle.

5. *Your children.* Choosing whether to have two or six children or choosing to have them when you are twenty or thirty affects your life moderately.

Minor Decisions

Minor decisions are made dozens of times a day. If minor decisions are made "to the glory of God" (Col. 3:16–17) and in conformity to His principles, the net result will have a positive effect on your life. These decisions, which are endless, include the following:

1. Which church service should you attend next Sunday?
2. Which store will you shop in?
3. Where should you buy your next car?
4. How can you find an honest orthodontist?
5. What should you do about the teenager your son is hanging around with?

Most miserable people, including many Christians, feel wretched because they make too many bad decisions—or, at best, second-rate choices. God is interested in helping you with all these decisions because He loves you. Some Christians allow Him to help them only with the major choices, while they make the minor decisions. That's usually why their life falls below the level of success and satisfaction that our Lord intended for them.

Learning the Hard Way

One day I walked into the family grocery store owned by one of our church members. Noticing a "Sold" sign in the window, I soon discovered Walt had sold the store to a buyer who offered him more than he could refuse. When I asked Walt if he had prayed about this decision, he replied, "No, I didn't." Naturally I asked why he hadn't asked God's advice about this matter. Selling a family business seemed like a major decision to me. His response was interesting. "Oh, I don't trouble God with ordinary decisions like that. I just ask His help in making the important ones. The ordinary decisions I make myself."

Within two months I was back in his store. The

buyer had cheated him, and only with much legal maneuvering and loss of money was Walt able to regain his business. It took over two years for him to recoup his loss and get the store back in shape to sell the second time. At that point, when I spotted another "For Sale" sign, I facetiously asked, "Have you prayed about it this time, Walt?"

He responded with a smile, "You bet I did! I don't intend to make that mistake again."

God wants us to bring all our requests to Him, particularly those that have the greatest influence on our lives. That's what He means by the passage in Proverbs: "In *all* your ways acknowledge Him, and *He shall direct your paths*" (Prov. 3:6 NKJV, emphasis added). Sometimes He will let us fall on our face, as He did my friend Walt, to convince us that He really is interested in every detail.

Summary

We tend to think that because God is the Master Creator of heaven and earth, He's too busy to be interested in the commonplace activities of our lives. In other words, our minds limit God to human abilities. Although humans may be restricted in their capacity to perform multiple tasks, God's "computer" is limitless. He is able to "do all things well," and that includes hearing our cry whenever we look in faith to Him. Remember, our Lord declares that He feeds the birds, takes care of the lilies in the field, and has even counted the hairs of our head (Matt. 6:25–34; 10:30). If God keeps watch over the dependent creatures in His world, how much *more* will He attend to the needs of His own children?

You are important to God! That truth must grip your

heart. His Word tells us that we are precious and valuable to Him.

You'll make many decisions that seem appropriate at the time without specifically praying for guidance. It's best, however, to start each day by committing yourself to God for direction, insuring that He will guide your paths, your steps, and every decision. Here's a good practice to follow: the more important the decision, the more specifically and earnestly you will seek the Lord's direction in the choices to be made. And before pursuing God's leading for your future, gain a basic understanding of His will for your present.

What We Already Know About God's Will

When we want to know the will of God about a particular situation, the first question we must ask ourselves is, "What do I *already know* about God's will for me?" Until we understand and obey God's known will, we will not discover His will for specific situations.

Where do we learn about God's will? From His Word, where He has carefully laid out guidelines for living. Personally, I don't believe you can find the will of God without consulting the Bible—or the advice of a friend who knows it. Yet many Christians make major decisions and try to find God's specific will for their life without even consulting Scripture. In fact, finding God's will is usually not difficult if we know and follow His clearly defined guidelines.

God has already revealed six commands that He wants us to obey. These commands are prerequisites to finding God's will in specific areas of our lives. If we ignore these commands, we'll never discover His will. If we obey them, we'll usually find that doing His will, even in this complex area, is really not difficult.

The helpful Scripture passages that reveal God's will fall into two categories: *commands* we all must keep and *principles* for finding God's specific individual will. The Ten Commandments, for example, were given for all people to obey. In addition He has written into His Word six commands that are specifically identified as "the will of God." Before you even try to discover God's individual or specific will for your life, you should have these six commands clearly in mind and practice. Personally, I find it's futile to expect God to give me specific direction unless I'm already obeying His revealed commands.

It Is God's Will That You Be Saved (2 Peter 3:9)

We read in 2 Peter 3:9 that "The Lord is not . . . willing that any should perish but that all should come to repentance" (NKJV). You probably thought I would quote John 3:16, because it describes the extent of God's love that would impel Him to give His only begotten Son for our salvation. But as wonderful as that thought is, it doesn't tell us *why* God loves us. The Bible clarifies that God created mankind for eternal life, and it is His will that all people be saved. In fact, 2 Peter 3:9 specifies that anyone who perishes does so against the will of God. Matthew 18:14 affirms this thought: "Even so it is not the will of your Father who is in heaven that one of these little ones should perish" (NKJV). Passages such as John 1:12–13 and 1 Timothy 2:3–4 further express God's will for our salvation.

In short, then, the first prerequisite to finding God's

will is salvation. If you aren't saved by being born again through faith in His Son and His finished work on the cross, then it's hopeless to try to find the will of God. Please settle that matter before you proceed!

It's important for you to burn this concept into your mind, not only to guarantee at the outset that you are one of His children, but also to assure yourself that God does have a will for your life. If He wants you to be saved—and He does—then He obviously has designed a plan for your life—and believe me, it's a good one!

Be Controlled by His Word and Spirit
(Ephesians 5:18–21; Colossians 3:16–17)

The second prerequisite to finding God's will is that we "walk in the Spirit" (Gal. 5:16a NKJV), meaning we should live in the control of His Spirit. Paul warned the Ephesian Christians, "Do not be unwise, but *understand what the will of the Lord is.* And do not be drunk with wine, in which is dissipation; but be filled with the Spirit" (Eph. 5:17–18 NKJV, emphasis added).

Although this may be the Bible's most important command to Christians, it is often the least obeyed. Verse 17 warns that the Christian who doesn't walk in the Spirit or isn't filled with the Spirit is "unwise." Many Christians view being filled with the Spirit as optional. Some who sincerely try to find the will of God fail to realize that they must first be filled with the Spirit. Identifying God's specific will in a given situation requires being sensitive to the leading of His Spirit.

How to Be Filled with the Spirit

When you were born again, God's Holy Spirit came into your life. God's Spirit wants to fill you, or control you, as verse 18 suggests. Just as a drunk is controlled by wine or alcohol, so the child of God should be controlled by the Holy Spirit.

How do we let the Spirit control us? The answer, according to a comparison of Ephesians 5:18–6:9 and Colossians 3:16–4:1, is to be filled with the Word of God. It's impossible to be filled with the Spirit on a lasting basis without being filled with the Word of God, for the Holy Spirit wrote the Word of God. As Scripture tells us, "Holy men of God spoke as they were moved by the Holy Spirit" (2 Peter 1:21b NKJV).

Recently I encountered a businessman who wanted to know how to find God's will. He seemed a bit annoyed when I asked him how long it had been since he had read the Bible for himself. He thought a minute and replied, "Except for church services, I haven't read it in several weeks." Frankly, I consider it a waste of his time and mine to seek God's will until he spends more time reading God's Word.

Examine carefully the results of the Spirit-filled life (Eph. 5 and 6) and the Word-filled life (Col. 3 and 4) in the chart below, and you will find they are identical.

Spirit-Filled Life		**Word-Filled Life**
Ephesians 5–6		*Colossians 3–4*
5:19	A song in your heart	3:16
5:20	A thanksgiving attitude	3:17
5:21–22	A submissive spirit Wives submit	3:18
5:25	Husbands love wives	3:19
6:1	Children obey parents	3:20
6:4	Fathers don't provoke Parents nurture children	3:21
6:5	Servants obey	3:22
6:6	Please God, not men	3:22
6:6	Do the will of God	3:23
6:9	Masters—sincerity	4:1

An Obvious Conclusion

Obviously, the Spirit-filled life and the Word-filled life are identical! If you want to be filled with the Spirit, then allow the Word of God to permeate your mind and heart, for through His Word, God fills our minds with His thoughts. We can't elicit God's thoughts from the world (our culture), the flesh (our old nature), or the devil (our enemy). To find God's will, we must learn to think God's thoughts. But to think His thoughts, we must be filled with His Word.

Many Christians make bad decisions because their minds are filled not with God's Word but with the world and its system. They then justify their bad decisions by saying, "I felt right about it" or "it seemed right at the time." The problem is not that they're not believers but that their minds were not filled with the Word of God.

If you'd like practical help in filling your mind with God's Word, I recommend my book, *How to Study the Bible for Yourself.** In it I offer several practical suggestions for Bible reading and study, along with some helpful charts that make Bible study interesting.

In the meantime, I suggest that you begin reading small books of the New Testament every day for thirty days. Start with Philippians, 1 John, Colossians, or your favorite book. Or divide the gospel of John into four sections of five chapters (the last section will be six), reading each section daily for one month—it takes only about twenty minutes a day. Within six months you'll have your mind filled with God's Word. Sin will lose its attraction to you, and you'll find it easier to discern God's will.

---

*Tim LaHaye, *How to Study the Bible for Yourself* (Eugene, Oregon: Harvest House, 1976).

Love God and Surrender to His Will
(Matthew 22:37)

The third prerequisite to finding God's will is to surrender to Him even before you know His will. The first commandment, according to our Lord, is that you "love the Lord your God with all your heart and with all your soul and with all your mind" (Matt. 22:37). Such comprehensive love for God naturally results in total submission.

That surrender was clearly described in the words of the apostle Paul, "I beseech you therefore, brethren, by the mercies of God, that you present your bodies a living sacrifice, holy, acceptable to God, which is your reasonable service. And do not be conformed to this world, but be transformed by the renewing of your mind, that you may prove what is that good and acceptable and perfect *will of God*" (Rom. 12:1–2 NKJV, emphasis added). All mortals have serious problems submitting their wills to God's will. He knows we are all rebellious by nature, which is why we have difficulty loving Him to the point of surrendering our bodies and minds to Him. Such surrender begins with the will.

What do the great men and women in the Bible have in common? Their love for God caused them to surrender to His will for their life, and their success can be measured in direct proportion to their surrender. For confirmation of that fact, read the biographies of Noah, Abraham, Moses, Joshua, Hannah, Esther, Elijah, David, Daniel—the list is endless. It continues into the New Testament with the Virgin Mary, Peter, John, Paul, and many others, then marches throughout almost 2000 years of church history with Wycliffe, Knox, Wesley, Moody, Finney, Goforth, and millions more.

Paul's words in Romans 12:1–2 (cited above)

contain perhaps the best-known challenge to present your body totally to God's will. This is not just a prayer; it's an attitude that you formalize into a prayer. And it should be done *before* you know the specific details of God's will for a particular situation. In essence you are telling God in advance, "Dear Lord, before You even reveal Your will, I am committed to doing it." That is implied in David's classic prayer, "Open my eyes, that I may see wondrous things from Your law" (Ps. 119:18 NKJV). As he approached God's Word, David affirmed: "Even before You reveal to me out of Your Word what You want me to do, I'm committed to doing it." That kind of attitude always leads to success in finding God's specific will.

A couple came in for counseling after visiting a Christian counseling center, explaining, "They gave us a battery of psychological tests. Our counselor told us that we were so hopelessly mismatched that we ought to get a divorce" (three children notwithstanding). It wasn't difficult to find the solution to their problem. But I needed to know in advance whether or not they were committed to doing God's will—which, surprisingly enough, they said they were. Since they had no biblical grounds for divorce (adultery), I confronted them with the words of 1 Corinthians 7:27, "Are you bound to a wife? Do not seek to be loosed" (NKJV). It took some time for them to find happiness in marriage, but it all began with advanced commitment to God's will—even before they knew what it was.

Study the following two verses in which God promises to reveal His will. Notice that these promises presuppose that the person seeking God's will *is already committed to doing it.*

> I will instruct you and teach you in the way you should go; I will guide you with My eye (Ps. 32:8 NKJV).

> Your ears shall hear a word behind you, saying, "This is the way, walk in it," whenever you turn to the right hand or whenever you turn to the left (Isa. 30:21 NKJV).

Personally, I doubt God gives such guidance to Christians whom He knows will not heed His voice. If you really want to know God's will, surrender to Him before He reveals it.

You can surrender gladly to God's will because you can trust that His will is good. Because He is a loving heavenly Father, you never need to worry about His design for your life. He certainly will direct your life more successfully than you can. The best bargain I ever made was when I surrendered my life totally to God. He has done with it "exceedingly abundantly above all that [I could ever] ask or think" (Eph. 3:20a NKJV).

He may not direct you in your path of preference, but be assured that His way is always, in the long run, the best way. As Paul reminds us, "He who did not spare His own Son, but delivered Him up for us all, how shall He not with Him also freely give us all things?" (Rom. 8:32 NKJV). A God who sacrificed His only Son for your salvation may be trusted to keep your best interests in view, both in this life and the life to come.

Live a Sanctified (Holy) Life
(1 Thessalonians 4:3–6)

The fourth prerequisite to finding the will of God is living a sanctified life. Paul defines what this sanctified life should be like in his letter to the Thessalonians:

> For this is the will of God, your sanctification: that
> you should abstain from sexual immorality; that
> each of you should know how to possess his own
> vessel in sanctification and honor, not in passion of
> lust, like the Gentiles who do not know God; that
> no one should take advantage of and defraud his
> brother in this matter (1 Thess. 4:3–6a NKJV).

A man once stopped me after a Family Life Seminar and asked for advice. "I'm a Spirit-filled Christian, I attend a Spirit-filled church, and I'm trying to decide if God wants me to divorce my wife so I can marry the woman I'm living with."

After recovering from shock, I responded, "Wait a minute. Let me straighten something out. You're not filled with the Holy Spirit!"

Usually I'm not that dogmatic, but in this instance I felt it was the only way to get through to this man. He wanted to know God's will about his love life, but he wasn't willing to follow God's will as it is already clearly revealed through Scripture.

When we don't live a holy life, we are completely out of His will. Sanctification isn't some special holy life God has reserved for super saints; it's His will for all believers. For that reason, let's take a look at the three characteristics of that holy or sanctified life, as Paul outlined it in 1 Thessalonians 4:3–6.

Abstain from Sexual Immorality

Next to self-preservation, sex is the most powerful force in life. It's not an inherently evil drive, for through it God wants us to propagate the race. But He wants us to control our sex drive—not let it control us.

Don't be surprised if sexual temptation becomes your biggest problem in living the Christian life. It always has been. That's why the apostle Paul, in his catalog of eighteen sins in Galatians 5:19–21, lists four sexual sins first; they *are* first!

If sexual temptation was awesome in the first century, just think what it is today. Our humanistic culture is saturated with sexual immorality, as reflected in advertising, sex-education classes without moral values, and government-sponsored "safe sex" campaigns that encourage fornication if it's done with proper precaution against disease.

In the will of God, sex can be the most beautiful and satisfying of all life's experiences. God's provision for sexual expression, however, is only within the confines of marriage. If you take time to study the Bible's view of sexual involvement, you'll find that every time the Bible refers to sex in marriage, it is good and holy; each time sexual expression is mentioned out of marriage, it is condemned or forbidden. That's why I could be so dogmatic with the young man mentioned above.

A Christian woman came to talk to me about the guilt trip laid on her because she wouldn't become sexually involved with the men she dated. She needed a pastor's encouragement that her responsibility was to do right, no matter what, and that meant keeping herself sexually pure. I reminded her that any man who might be God's will for her would appreciate her resolution and respect her for it. I further urged her to stop looking for a partner and to let God send one. I told her, "When God introduces you to Mr. Right, you'll be glad you waited." When she questioned whether God would ever send her a partner, I reminded her, "If he doesn't, you're better off without Mr. Wrong!"

I'm happy to say that she waited two years, dated a few men, and then he came—Mr. Right, whose wife had died two years before, just about the time we had our talk. He later confided that he had prayed for over a year that God would send him a godly wife with whom he could share his life—and one who would be a good mother to his three girls. Today they have a beautiful Christian home.

As someone has said, "God gives the best to those who leave the choice to Him." But that involves living a sanctified sex life!

Possess Your Body in Sanctification and Honor

According to verse 4, God wills "that each of you should know how to possess his own vessel [body] in sanctification and honor, not in passion like the Gentiles." God wants your body! He has never made a secret of that. All through Scripture and church history, He repeatedly asks His children, "Who is going to use your body?" Remember, Satan is a liar. He doesn't say, "I want your body." Instead he advises, "Do your own thing. You don't need anyone up there telling you what to do." He always tempts us with rebellion. Of course, he fails to tell people that when they do their own will, they're really doing *his* will.

So you have to make a choice—not once, but throughout life. Who gets to use your body, Satan or God? You have only one body—and God wants it. But He doesn't claim it in its old, sin-filled condition—He insists that it be clean. We learn that lesson not only from this passage but also in Paul's advice to Timothy (2 Tim. 2:22).

The good news about this challenge is that you can do something about your sanctification. You can't change your looks, your intelligence quotient, or your talents, but you can determine your sanctification. Most of us presume that if only we had more talent or ability,

God would use us. God certainly values gifted people, but He puts a premium on clean vessels.

Verse 5 adds that now that we are saved, we shouldn't act like pagan Gentiles—in the "passion of lust"—as we did before we came to Christ. The world is given over to passion by cultivating lust. That's why pornography dealers get rich and why X-rated movies, TV shows, and videos are popular. They appeal to the lust of the flesh, or as modern judges label them, "prurient interests."

Passion is a normal, God-given drive fanned into a raging flame by indulgence in lustful thoughts or speech. Christians who would possess their bodies "in honor" must purify their minds by refusing to take in pornography or other suggestive material. In addition, they must purge their minds of past lustful memories.

While ministering through an interpreter in a foreign country, I grew to appreciate the young man who was my "mouth" in his mother tongue. He was a Christian of only five years, married and a father. When he thought he could talk to me personally, he asked the question often voiced by men of my own country. "Before I became a Christian, I lived a 'macho lifestyle.' How do I rid myself of those thoughts that come back from time to time and ruin my walk with God?"

I explained to him that two steps are necessary to cleanse the mind, which is the key to subduing youthful lusts or any other kind of lusts. First, stop filling your mind with sexual stimuli; second, saturate it with the Word of God. Spend more time reading and memorizing His Word so that His Word within you will prevent you from sinning (Ps. 119:11). When you have possessed your mind and body in sanctification, watch for God to lead and use your life. Don't force Him to pass over your life because it's a dirty vessel.

That concept was illustrated early one Monday morning when I stepped to the kitchen sink. The previous night's guests had used every drinking vessel we owned, with one exception. Even the fancy cut stemware the church gave us one Christmas, which I always accused Bev of saving for her next husband, had been dirtied. As beautiful as they were, I passed over them all and reached back into the cupboard for the gnarled plastic cup our youngest child had chewed on while teething.

Why did I reach for that ugly old cup? It was clean! For the same reason, God often bypasses many talented Christians and selects an "ordinary vessel"—because he or she is clean.

Deal Honestly with Others

Within all human beings lies the temptation to take advantage of or defraud other people. We've all been tempted to cheat or lie to gain advantage over someone else. But the Christian should be different. We are our brother's keeper! Instead of being takers, we should be givers. If telling the truth will cost us money in a business deal, we should be willing to pay it—just because we're honest. It's ludicrous to lie or cheat, then piously ask God to help us find His will for our life. He demands that we tell the truth, that we show concern for other people. That's part of our sanctification.

Obey Legitimate Authority
(1 Peter 2:13–15)

The fifth prerequisite to finding God's will is to submit to those in authority over you. The apostle Peter puts it this way: "Therefore submit yourselves to every ordinance of man for the Lord's sake, whether to the king as supreme, or to governors, as to those who are sent by him for the punishment of evildoers and for the praise of those who do good. *For this is the will of God* that by doing good you may put to silence the ignorance of foolish men" (1 Peter 2:13–15 NKJV, emphasis added).

God's will calls for Christians to be obedient to government authorities, laws, even employers, as long as their requirements don't cause us to violate the higher law of God. Throughout history, Christians have been tempted to violate the law to accomplish something "good." But this is forbidden, for it hinders our Christian witness. If we disobey a duly constituted authority, we have violated God's will.

That doesn't mean that God approves the laws of all governments. In fact, historically, most governments have been evil and hurtful to people, which explains why Scripture often refers to them as "beasts." Nevertheless, if everyone defied the law, we would have anarchy, which would make it even more difficult to accomplish God's primary will—to preach the gospel to all the world.

Christians should be examples to other people in obeying the law. We should serve as models in the way we pay our taxes, drive our cars, settle our indebtedness, and respect the rights of others. If governments pass laws that we don't agree with, we have the liberty to work to change them. And we should. In the meantime, unless the laws force us to disobey one of God's laws, we should obey them.

Take the subject of abortion, which was legalized in 1973. Just because a majority of the Supreme Court voted to legalize the murder of the unborn, we shouldn't feel compelled to agree with or participate in its decision. Doctors and nurses have been known to refuse to perform abortions because they appealed to a higher law: "You shall not murder" (Exod. 20:13).

On the other hand, some ill-advised people have taken the law into their own hands, bombing abortion clinics. Fortunately, no one has been killed, but such activity is wrong; it violates the law. The energy of such people should be aimed at registering more Christians to vote and working on behalf of candidates who share their moral values so that unjust laws can be changed legally. In fact, if all Christians voted for morally committed candidates, we would eventually have enough members on the Supreme Court to reverse *Roe vs. Wade* and spare the 1.5 million unborn babies now being aborted each year. But that's a legitimate use of law, obeying the law to bring about change. Taking the law into your own hands is not God's will.

If you find it intolerable to work for someone, you should nevertheless obey that person or ask God for another place of employment. In fact, your feelings of discontent may be God's Spirit leading you to look elsewhere. On the other hand, God may want to use your spirit of submission in the face of adverse circumstances as a testimony. As Peter said, "For it is better, *if it is the will of God,* to suffer for doing good than for doing evil" (1 Peter 3:17 NKJV, emphasis added).

The apostle Paul also makes it clear that we should not only execute the will of God but also do it "from the heart," not as "men-pleasers" but as God-pleasers (Eph. 6:6–7 NKJV).

Be a Thankful Person
(1 Thessalonians 5:6–18)

The sixth prerequisite to finding the will of God is having a mental attitude of thankfulness. The Scripture tells us, "In everything give thanks; *for this is the will of God* in Christ Jesus for you" (1 Thess. 5:18 NKJV, emphasis added). In other places, Scripture teaches us to "rejoice ever more," "pray with thanksgiving," and "be thankful." But this verse from 1 Thessalonians specifically links thanksgiving to the will of God.

By nature, none of us is thankful. But when we walk in the Spirit, we'll respond with a thankful attitude. When we gripe or chafe, we're not in the will of God. It's easier for God to lead us to His specific will when we possess a thanksgiving attitude. I've met people who were constant self-pitying complainers, probably induced by their temperament and developed by use into a lifetime habit. Such a habit must be replaced by the giving of thanks if we wish to enjoy God's will. If you or someone you love has a problem with maintaining a thankful heart in the midst of adverse circumstances, make this a priority with God.

You may wonder why I saved this command of God as the last prerequisite to discovering His will. It's because I've watched several Christians do everything else right yet nullify God's will by their very human but ungrateful attitude. By developing a mental attitude of thanksgiving, you are opening your heart and mind for God's specific direction for your life.

Summary

These six important prerequisites to finding God's will must be viewed as commands to obey, not options to consider. These, of course, do not total all of God's commands revealed in the Bible, but you'll find that all other commands will fit neatly under one of these major categories.

In addition to revealed commands, numerous principles in the Word will establish your walk with Him, another reason for reading and studying the Scriptures regularly. The better you know the Word, the more easily you will discover God's will for your life—*if* you are willing to do it.

▷ *And remember this, the Spirit of God will never lead you to violate His Word—for He wrote it! God is not the author of confusion.*

4

God Has
a Specific Will
for Your Life

Over 50 million people in our generation have heard this statement: "God loves you and has a wonderful plan for your life!" You'll recognize that as the first of the famous four spiritual laws, designed by Dr. Bill Bright of Campus Crusade for Christ (CCC). Bill told me that many have heard that first law through the ministry of the 16,000 CCC representatives throughout the world and through the millions they have trained to use it. Bill and I met "by chance" in the Chicago airport as I was researching this book and after I had decided to use that introduction to this chapter. I had a much smaller figure in mind, but Bill knows the far-reaching extent of this worldwide ministry. Personally, I find it exciting that so many millions have been confronted with the good news of God's loving plan for them—and that many millions have responded.

With over 5 billion people on planet earth, does it

seem incredible that God has established a plan for *your* life and mine? But He has! The Bible is very clear about that. Consider, for instance, "We do not cease to pray for you, and to ask *that you may be filled with the knowledge of His will* in all wisdom and spiritual understanding; that you may have a walk worthy of the Lord, fully pleasing Him, being fruitful in every good work and increasing in the knowledge of God" (Col. 1:9–10 NKJV, emphasis added; see also Eph. 4:1).

God not only has a plan for our lives, but He also wants to reveal that plan to us. In fact, our purpose in being on this earth is to do God's will. One of the important questions of the old Calvinist catechism still used by some churches today asks, "What is the chief purpose of man?" The answer: "To glorify God" (based on Rev. 4:11).

The Universal Will of God

God's universal will, sometimes called His moral will, is what He expects all His children to do. We examined six aspects of that universal will in the previous chapter. His universal will is not to be confused with His individual will for your life. The individual or specific will of God is His tailor-made plan just for you. The following chart, which lists some of the six major commands God has already given in His Word regarding His will, plus the Ten Commandments, comprise His universal will for all believers.

As you'll see, if you want to know God's individual will, first do His moral or universal will. Once you obey His universal will, you'll find it easier to discern His specific will.

The Christian's Life Chart

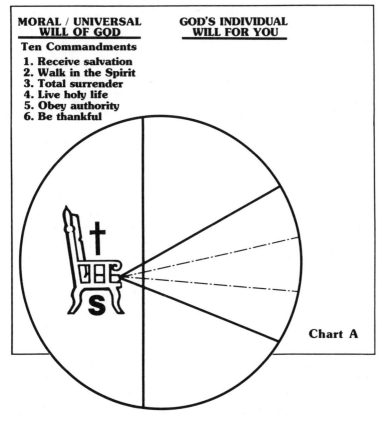

MORAL / UNIVERSAL WILL OF GOD

GOD'S INDIVIDUAL WILL FOR YOU

Ten Commandments

1. Receive salvation
2. Walk in the Spirit
3. Total surrender
4. Live holy life
5. Obey authority
6. Be thankful

Chart A

Beware the New Fad

Recently a somewhat controversial book emerged, suggesting, in essence, that God doesn't have an individual or specific will for each Christian; the book suggests that once you've responded to the moral or universal will of God, you then can use your own judgment and proceed as you wish. The author theorizes that Spirit-filled Christians are capable of making the best of the choices before them, so that doing God's will is just doing what seems best to you at the time. In fairness to those who hold this new theory, they likewise believe that we should be filled with the Word and the Spirit, maintaining an attitude of obedience to God. And while they don't seem to advocate self-will, unfortunately, that may logically follow the practice of making your own choices. If we no longer practice the concept that "in all [our] ways [we must] acknowledge Him, and He shall direct [our] paths" (Prov. 3:6 NKJV), it's only a matter of time before we begin to function independently from God. He shrouds His will in the first place so that we must seek Him continually on a personal basis. Why else would Paul enjoin, "pray without ceasing," unless we needed moment-by-moment direction, supply, protection, and power?

After examining this new fad, I'm reminded of the warning of the late Dr. Harry Ironside, my favorite Bible teacher. He taught, "Beware of what is new, for it may not be true." I found this new theory, advocated by very sincere people, to be not only potentially dangerous but also unscriptural. While they debunk the traditional view of finding God's will, they also ignore or twist Scripture to fit their purposes, flying in the face of God's dealings with hundreds of biblical figures who ignored important teachings of Scripture. As we'll see, God's dealings with men and women throughout the Bible reflect an individual will for them. Their stories are included as examples to us, both good and bad, depending on their response to God's will.

God Has a Specific Will for You

Discovering God's specific will for our lives always begins with obedience to His known will. We know

from the Bible that God's will is for us to serve Him—
but we don't know where He *specifically* wants us to
serve. We know it is His will for us to "preach the
gospel to every creature" (Mark 16:15b)—but we don't
know where He *specifically* wants us to spread the
gospel. Scripture tells us to work, but it doesn't specify
place or occupation. We are instructed (for the most
part) to marry and have children, but we don't know
specifically whom we are to marry or how many
children we should have.

Bible Characters Who Discovered
God's Specific Will

God expects our pursuit of His individual will to be
a day-by-day experience of drawing nigh to Him for
direction through His Word and Holy Spirit, as illustrated in the lives of hundreds of Bible characters whom
God used. He structured a different plan for each one,
but He did have a plan.

For example, Adam and Eve were placed in the
Garden and told to be fruitful and multiply and people
the earth. God then instructed them to till the Garden.
He further explained that they could eat anything
except the fruit of the tree of the knowledge of good and
evil. The first steps in God's will for them were to bear
children and to tend the Garden; then He tested their
obedience—a test they failed. But notice how specific
God's will was for them!

Later God spoke to Noah, a godly man who had
found favor in the Lord's sight, even though he lived in
a corrupt society. God established a one-hundred-
twenty-year boat-building project for Noah, followed by
an animal-gathering project. Because of Noah's obedience, God used him to preserve all life, both animal and

human. For more than a century, then, Noah diligently followed God's will for him and his family.

A perusal of the Old Testament takes us through the labyrinth of God's specific will for Abraham, Isaac, Jacob, his sons (read Gen. 49), Joseph, Moses, Joshua, hundreds of prophets, priests, judges, King Saul, David the shepherd boy (who became king), Solomon, many other kings, housewives, mothers, sisters, and millions of Old Testament saints—and we haven't yet entered the domain of the New Testament!

Note the specific nature of His will for some of the New Testament saints. The apostle Paul is probably the clearest example. Several times he referred to the fact that he had been "called to be an apostle of Jesus Christ through the will of God" (1 Cor. 1:1 NKJV). You'll have to admit that Paul was given a decidedly specific assignment. Writing to Timothy about this assignment, Paul said of our Lord, "He counted me faithful, putting me into the ministry" (1 Tim. 1:12b NKJV). For further evidence of this specific will of God for Paul and others, consider the selection of Paul and Barnabas for the first missionary journey (Acts 13:1–2) or the famous Macedonian "call" of Acts 16:10. God ordained Paul to open Europe to the gospel and to conclude his days in Rome—again, a specific pattern, which the apostle completed.

Or take the example of the evangelist Philip, who in the midst of preaching a "crusade," as we would call it, was specifically instructed to go down to the desert, where he met the Ethiopian and led him to Christ. One can hardly get more specific than that.

Others Who Discovered God's Specific Will

And don't conclude that God used only the people mentioned in Scripture. I'm confident that when we get to heaven, we'll learn about "the Acts" of the many other first-century disciples, like the early church fathers. And after them came millions of faithful servants right up to our present day.

God has a plan for each of His children—a different plan for each life. Some He calls to be housewives and mothers, others to be shoe cobblers, who, like William Carey, may be summoned from the shoemaker's shop to open a foreign country to modern missions. God led Roger Sherman, the godly Connecticut Sunday school teacher and deacon, to leave his cobbler shop, enter law school, then proceed into politics, where he distinguished himself as the only American who signed all four of our nation's founding documents and was influential in writing our Constitution.

The life of James Madison is another example of God's specific will for a person's life. Recognizing his intelligence and spiritual sensitivity, Madison's parents were not surprised when he announced he felt led to study for the ministry. To protect him from the heretics on the faculty of the local denominational college, William and Mary, they sent him to Princeton. There Madison studied under the great preacher John Witherspoon, who just thirteen years earlier had left his Presbyterian church in Scotland to become president of a new American college. Witherspoon stamped his image of godliness and biblical law on nine of the fifty-five founding fathers who wrote our Constitution—including young James Madison, who had switched to the field of law and who probably had more influence on the Constitution's design than any other founder. Madison also introduced our Bill of Rights and became the nation's fourth President.

Coincidence? Not for a moment. The destiny of America would have been vastly different if God hadn't led John Witherspoon, the most influential legal authority in the colonies in 1776, to our shores. This is just one of hundreds of such stories from American history. Millions of unreported people were equally obedient to God and found His perfect will for their individual lives.

The history of Christianity is filled with stories of God's children who have walked through a lifetime of fulfilling His specific plan for their life—some to fame and fortune, most to obscurity and routine living, but all to fulfillment. God created a specific will for these believers, and their earthly success in God's eyes was determined by the extent to which they sought it and obeyed it. So is ours.

What About Us?

God calls us to specific tasks too. Ephesians tells us that to build and edify His church, the Lord has appointed or called "some to be apostles, some prophets, some evangelists, and some pastors and teachers" (Eph. 4:11 NKJV). Obviously our callings vary—some to the ministry, some to education (both Christian and secular), others to medicine, law, politics, construction, management, and a host of other specific callings. As we'll see, the key to knowing the will of God is finding and doing it.

When we hear success stories, we primarily celebrate the final results. We rarely learn about the tedious training, the discouragements, the waiting, or the thousands of decisions that had to be made, many times on one's knees in prayer. We probably never hear about the disappointments, the loss of focus, the inclination to quit under fire. But be assured, those successful saints were just as human as you are. Though not perfect, they did register implicit obedience to God.

The key to success in fulfilling God's will for your life—particularly in this crazy, complex world in which we live—involves faithfulness in knowing His Word, following His Holy Spirit, and finishing today's tasks. As a result, when God opens the next door of His leading, you'll be prepared to walk through it.

And be sure also of this: those successful saints you admire were faithful in the small things long before they ever accomplished the big things for God. I've never known anyone to start out at the top and succeed. That would defy one of our Lord's principles: the person who is "faithful over a few things, I will make you ruler over many things" (Matt. 25:21b NKJV). The key to experiencing the impressive, exciting episodes in God's will is to be faithful in completing the many little tasks.

Additional Scriptures to Study

As a means of further illustrating that God's Word affirms a specific will for your life, study the following verses carefully.

Created for Good Works

"For we are His workmanship, created in Christ Jesus for good works, which God prepared beforehand that we should walk in them" (Eph. 2:10 NKJV).

God's Way

"Your ears shall hear a word behind you, saying, 'This is the way, walk in it,' whenever you turn to the right hand or whenever you turn to the left" (Isa. 30:21 NKJV).

God Will Guide You to His Way

"I will instruct you and teach you in the way you should go; I will guide you with My eye" (Ps. 32:8 NKJV).

Because of His mercy, He leads and guides His children. "For He who has mercy on them will lead them, even by the springs of water will He guide them" (Isa. 49:10b).

He guides all who are humble and obedient (See Ps. 25:9–10).

God teaches and leads us how to go: "I am the Lord" (See Isa. 48:17).

Obedience is the surest and only way to happiness (See Ps. 119:1–5).

5

Three Levels
of God's Will

Present your bodies a living sacrifice, holy, acceptable to God, which is your reasonable service. And
do not be conformed to this world, but be transformed by the renewing of your mind, that you may
prove what is that *good* and *acceptable* and *perfect*
will of God. (Rom. 12:1–2 NKJV, emphasis added)

Most Bible teachers accept the three words,
"good," "acceptable," and "perfect" as modifiers of the
one will of God. By contrast, I view them as *three levels*
of that one will. While it is essentially true that God has
but one basic will—His "perfect" or complete will—
"good" and "acceptable" describe God's will for the
people who fall into sin but then repent and still desire
to do God's basic will.

An examination of the three words will reveal
they're not the same. Instead, they graduate upward in
value. Consider some of the meanings for these Greek
words:

> *Good*—fair, valuable, and of benefit
> *Acceptable*—well-pleasing, agreeable
> *Perfect*—complete, mature, finished

Paul uses the word "perfect" in relation to our need to come "to a perfect man, to the measure of the stature of the fullness of Christ" (Eph. 4:13b NKJV). That is, he desired all Christians to grow spiritually mature so they could do the complete will of God. And as you know, he was the model of one who fulfilled the will and purpose of God for his life. His supreme desire was to do God's will.

Many Christians ultimately carry out God's good will, others His acceptable will. But all too few fulfill God's supreme desire, which requires that we start early in our Christian life and walk in consistent obedience to Him *most* of our life to complete His perfect will for our lives. Satisfying God's perfect will requires almost a lifetime of faithful obedience to Him, or at least that we do not make a major decision when out of His will.

The Three Levels of God's Will

As you examine Chart B, which represents the circle of life, note on the right the three levels of God's specific will for your life. I've borrowed my friend Bill Bright's famous throne to designate your free will, which determines everything you do.

Notice first that you can't even move into the will-of-God zone until Christ (cross) is in control of your will and until your self-life (S) is put under the throne in the servant's position. As long as you allow the Lord to make the decisions in your life, you'll always obey God's universal will. And if you function throughout life

The Obedient Christian

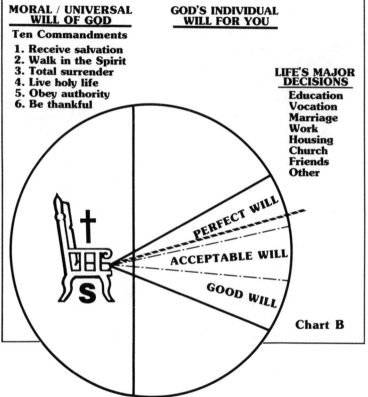

MORAL / UNIVERSAL WILL OF GOD

Ten Commandments

1. Receive salvation
2. Walk in the Spirit
3. Total surrender
4. Live holy life
5. Obey authority
6. Be thankful

GOD'S INDIVIDUAL WILL FOR YOU

LIFE'S MAJOR DECISIONS

Education
Vocation
Marriage
Work
Housing
Church
Friends
Other

PERFECT WILL

ACCEPTABLE WILL

GOOD WILL

Chart B

with Christ in control, you'll automatically complete God's perfect will.

If you take the decision-making control back into your own hands, however, Christ is no longer in control of your life. Instead, self (S) is on the throne, affecting the decisions of *its* choice. If self yields to the appetites of the flesh and violates God's moral law, you immediately cease to do both God's individual will and His universal will. Chart C illustrates your condition.

The Disobedient Christian

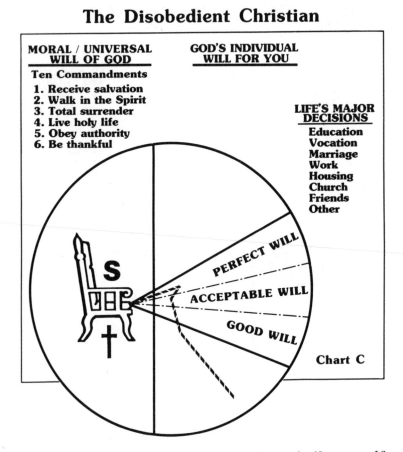

MORAL / UNIVERSAL WILL OF GOD

Ten Commandments

1. Receive salvation
2. Walk in the Spirit
3. Total surrender
4. Live holy life
5. Obey authority
6. Be thankful

GOD'S INDIVIDUAL WILL FOR YOU

LIFE'S MAJOR DECISIONS

Education
Vocation
Marriage
Work
Housing
Church
Friends
Other

PERFECT WILL

ACCEPTABLE WILL

GOOD WILL

Chart C

Hopefully, you don't stay in this rebellious, self-willed condition very long, for such a position seriously jeopardizes your opportunity of fulfilling God's perfect will for your life. Instead, let's assume that you recognize the error of your way and return to God in repentance. He instantly forgives and restores you to your previous state. *If* you didn't make any life-changing decisions and *if* you didn't remain in that selfish condition too long, you can yet fulfill God's perfect will, as reflected in Chart D.

The Restored Christian

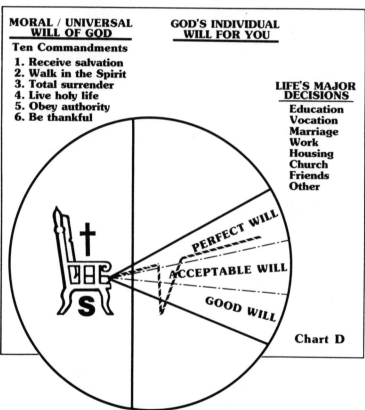

MORAL / UNIVERSAL WILL OF GOD

Ten Commandments
1. Receive salvation
2. Walk in the Spirit
3. Total surrender
4. Live holy life
5. Obey authority
6. Be thankful

GOD'S INDIVIDUAL WILL FOR YOU

LIFE'S MAJOR DECISIONS
Education
Vocation
Marriage
Work
Housing
Church
Friends
Other

PERFECT WILL

ACCEPTABLE WILL

GOOD WILL

Chart D

Now let's see what happened when a Christian young man rebelled, disobeyed the Lord, and refused to respond to the Holy Spirit's conviction within him or the remonstrances of his friends and family around him.

During my late teens, shortly after giving my life to the gospel ministry (which later proved to be God's perfect will for my life), I witnessed an unforgettable story. The most talented, best-looking young man in our church—I'll call him Ken—also was called to the ministry. Three years older than I, Ken started dating a young Christian woman in our church group. As they became more physically involved, he started to change. He came to church only sporadically, and he lost his involvement in the church group. Finally they announced a hasty wedding because the girl had become pregnant.

Ken was never the same. He repented, was restored, and became a policeman, but he abandoned all thoughts of entering the ministry. His spiritual life became a roller coaster, and he harbored resentment because he was prevented from doing God's perfect will. Eventually he committed suicide.

Ken's tragic story is in many ways the story of thousands of Christians who in moments of self-will violate God's moral laws and destroy their potential to do His perfect will. Ken's tragic end is graphically pictured in Chart E.

What should Ken have done? If he had been counseled properly and if he would have been willing to follow that counsel, he still could have accomplished God's acceptable will. We don't know, of course, whether or not the girl was right for him. But even if she were not, they could have found God's forgiveness and pursued God's acceptable will together. Ken probably never would have been able to accept a pastorate, although even that might have been possible if he'd gone to seminary and moved to another part of the country to serve God. The obligation to support a wife and new baby, however, made it impossible for him to get his training. Consequently, he missed God's call for his life, or, more accurately, he aborted God's perfect will for his life.

The Rebellious Christian (1)

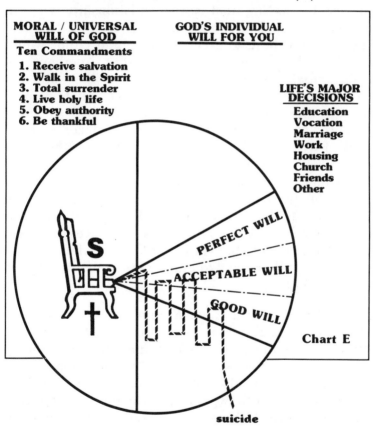

MORAL / UNIVERSAL WILL OF GOD

Ten Commandments

1. Receive salvation
2. Walk in the Spirit
3. Total surrender
4. Live holy life
5. Obey authority
6. Be thankful

GOD'S INDIVIDUAL WILL FOR YOU

LIFE'S MAJOR DECISIONS

Education
Vocation
Marriage
Work
Housing
Church
Friends
Other

S

PERFECT WILL

ACCEPTABLE WILL

GOOD WILL

Chart E

suicide

But even though Ken couldn't fulfill his original call to ministry, he still could have served God in a variety of ways. Like my friend, Assistant Chief Bob Vernon of the Los Angeles Police Department, Ken could have had a tremendous ministry in his job as a policeman. Over the years, even the *Los Angeles Times* accused Bob of being the influential person behind the 400-plus Christians recruited to the L.A.P.D.

Or what if Ken had complicated his life even further by having that sexual relationship with an unsaved girl and then marrying her? And let's assume she wasn't willing to accept Christ. She either would live with him in an unhappy situation—perhaps not even agreeing to raise his children in the faith that meant so much to him personally—or she might divorce him, further ensnaring his life. If Ken had sincerely repented, even after such catastrophic mistakes, and had walked with God the rest of his life, the best he could expect would be God's good will.

Don't misunderstand. God's good will is a worthy option for the Christian who has rebelled against the Lord and has made many major decisions during that rebellious time. Although the consequences will prohibit that person from ever doing God's perfect will, he or she can still proceed to either of the other two levels of God's will.

A Bad Story with a Good Ending

Let's look again at the story from chapter 1 of Fran, the woman with an unrepentant, unfaithful husband. If you remember, Fran had married an unsaved man, thus moving outside God's will. For many years she had lived a hell-on-earth experience, which is often the case when a believer is "unequally yoked together" with an unbeliever (2 Cor. 6:14a NKJV).

Obviously Fran had missed God's perfect will for her life. But in God's grace, her husband eventually had become a Christian, and as a result, Fran was able to experience God's acceptable will. This, however, was thwarted by her husband's infidelity after thirty years of marriage. When her husband divorced her, she wondered what she would do. What was God's will for her at this point in her life?

The Resubmitted Christian

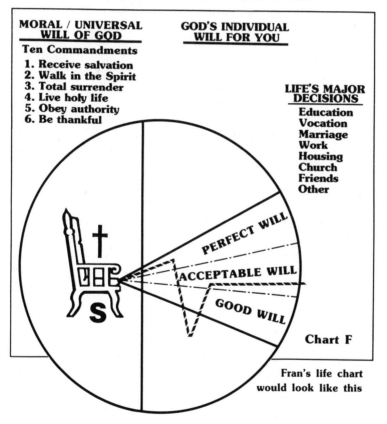

MORAL / UNIVERSAL WILL OF GOD

Ten Commandments

1. Receive salvation
2. Walk in the Spirit
3. Total surrender
4. Live holy life
5. Obey authority
6. Be thankful

GOD'S INDIVIDUAL WILL FOR YOU

LIFE'S MAJOR DECISIONS

Education
Vocation
Marriage
Work
Housing
Church
Friends
Other

PERFECT WILL

ACCEPTABLE WILL

GOOD WILL

Chart F

Fran's life chart would look like this

Fran received counseling from her pastor and from friends who knew the Scriptures. They advised her not to remarry but to "wait on the Lord" (Ps. 27:14 NKJV).

Although this was difficult for Fran to do, she obeyed the scriptural advice of her pastor and prayerfully waited for God to act. And He did. Listen to the rest of her story.

"Finally my husband renounced his wayward life, did not marry the woman he left me for, and renewed his commitment to the Lord and his family. Praise the Lord! We were remarried last year. Our grandchildren loved the wedding. Our son-in-law performed the ceremony! We are in a very loving, forgiving church, and they have loved him back into the great Christian body."

While we thrill at the outcome of this story and the loving nature of Fran's congregation, we shouldn't be blind to the heartache and suffering she endured for years, and we shouldn't overlook the shame and reproach this man's sin brought to the cause of Christ. Even though the story turned out well, we should remember that Fran will never fulfill God's perfect will. She probably will settle for God's good will the rest of her life. Admittedly, she gained a measure of happiness in doing God's good will, but it's not the perfect plan the Master had prepared for her life. (See Chart F.)

Living Sacrifices

Basically, though not exclusively, Paul's instructions to prove the good and acceptable and perfect will of God relate to vocational life. Marriage, lifestyle, and many other elements, however, are also identified with God's will. Paul challenges you to present your body to God as a "living sacrifice." We are to be Christ's ambassadors. That doesn't mean everyone needs to be a missionary or a minister. It means that the Christian's primary vocation is to be Christ's ambassador—whether that person is a railroad crossing guard or a pilot.

I know people whose jobs may be dentistry or doctoring, but their primary vocation involves service as an ambassador for Christ. When they presented their lives to Christ unconditionally, He guided them into a lifetime pursuit of medicine. Here in Washington, D.C., I've met congresspeople, senators, and government workers whose primary life objective is to do God's perfect will. Their secondary vocational objective is politics. I've seen people who've committed their whole lives to Christ's service and are placed in jobs as lawyers, architects, businesspeople, homemakers and mothers, school teachers—the list is endless.

Each person looked for God's perfect will—and did it. But as we shall see, doing God's will vocationally will also involve many other areas of your life—your morals, marriage, standard of living, church life, etc.

Two Doctors Who "Blew It"

I remember praying with a handsome young pre-med student who was convinced that medicine was God's will for his life. I concurred. He was a 4.0 student who daily read the Word and constantly witnessed everywhere he went. He didn't feel led to become a medical missionary but often told me he'd like to support at least one missionary family when he established his practice. He also dreamed of visiting needy areas of the world for short-term medical missionary work. He was even looking for a fellow Christian doctor with whom to share his practice, one who would minister with him in strengthening the witness of the missionaries.

All of that changed, however, after he met an attractive, manipulative nurse while doing his intern-

The Rebellious Christian (2)

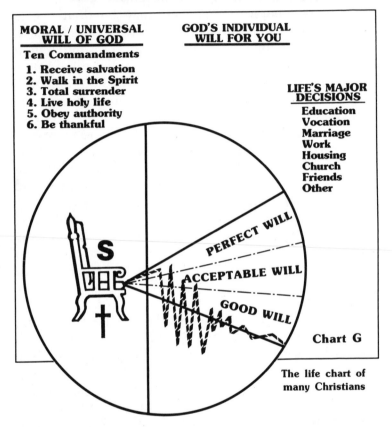

MORAL / UNIVERSAL WILL OF GOD

Ten Commandments

1. Receive salvation
2. Walk in the Spirit
3. Total surrender
4. Live holy life
5. Obey authority
6. Be thankful

GOD'S INDIVIDUAL WILL FOR YOU

LIFE'S MAJOR DECISIONS

Education
Vocation
Marriage
Work
Housing
Church
Friends
Other

S

PERFECT WILL

ACCEPTABLE WILL

GOOD WILL

Chart G

The life chart of many Christians

ship at a local hospital. She was a professing Christian but very carnal. Like so many marriageable young men, he was no match for a provocative female who had set her sights on him. His spiritual ardor seemed to fade as his libido intensified. They now have a Christian home, and he is a successful, respected professional in the community. But he's lost all thoughts of supporting missionaries or spending time on the mission field. During the time when he wasn't doing God's perfect will morally, he became "unequally yoked" with a carnal Christian. Instead of bringing her up to his previous level of dedication, she brought him down to her sphere of carnality.

I've counseled them for marital problems; unless they return to the Lord and rededicate their lives to God's perfect will, I give their marriage no better than a fifty-fifty chance of surviving for more than five years. He's beginning to resent her fiercely because of the way she has influenced him, and that is the handwriting on the wall. Chart G reflects his life circle.

An even more dreadful story concerns a classmate of mine from a Christian college. We played sports together and were very close until he decided that becoming a minister was his parents' decision; he wanted to be a rich and famous doctor. Against the advice and prayers of several friends, he left school to study medicine. In short, he rejected God's perfect will and headed down the path of misery and disappointment.

He married a woman who was hostile to Jesus Christ. To be sure, he became wealthy, but his residence in Vanity Fair led him into alcoholism, and he drank himself to death at age forty-six. All spiritual benefits in this life were forfeited because self-will superseded God's divine will. His life circle is pictured in Chart H.

God's Perfect Will and Major Decisions

It is always imperative that you are in the perfect-will-of-God attitude (one of complete surrender to Him) when making the major and most of the moderate decisions of life. If you make a minor decision when out of the will of God, it well might have harmful effects on your future—but it will probably not be life-threatening.

The Rebellious Christian (3)

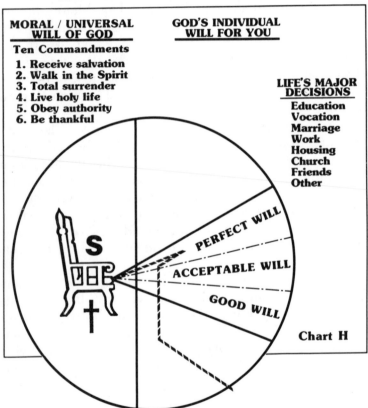

MORAL / UNIVERSAL WILL OF GOD

Ten Commandments

1. Receive salvation
2. Walk in the Spirit
3. Total surrender
4. Live holy life
5. Obey authority
6. Be thankful

GOD'S INDIVIDUAL WILL FOR YOU

LIFE'S MAJOR DECISIONS
Education
Vocation
Marriage
Work
Housing
Church
Friends
Other

S

PERFECT WILL

ACCEPTABLE WILL

GOOD WILL

Chart H

Obviously, the effects of a decision are influenced by the importance of that decision. Suppose, for instance, that while you're out of God's will, you buy a car you can't afford, take a hobby that has no real merit, or join the wrong club or organization. All these decisions can be amended. True, you may endure additional expense for a time, work several months or even years paying back unnecessary bills, or face extensive moving costs after quitting the wrong job. But in time, you can return to God's perfect will. If not, then the acceptable will of God is still open to you.

The key, of course, is the length of time you spend out of His perfect will before repenting and once again allowing Him to make the decisions of your life, particularly the major ones. That's why He challenges us, "In all your ways acknowledge [Me], and [I] will direct your paths" (Prov. 3:6 NKJV). Obedience to God's revealed will, which is His moral/universal will, is the first step to finding His individual will.

Practical Answers to Appropriate Questions

Whenever I present this theory, I'm confronted with several interesting questions. To save you a postage stamp, I'll include some of them here.

▷ *Is it possible to do God's perfect will for my life if I come to faith late in life?*

Evidently it is, for Paul gave that challenge to the Romans, who had been pagans before accepting Christ. They probably had lived their entire lives outside of God's moral or universal will. I would assume that God doesn't have a perfect will for anyone beyond a person's coming to faith in Christ. After that moment of salvation, God develops that perfect will, based on the person's age at the time of salvation. Obviously, it's not God's will for an eighty-five-year-old new convert on his deathbed to leave for Africa as a missionary. For the baby Christian who happens to be a convict on death row, God's will may be limited but perfect. Convicted criminals, after coming to faith, have had effective ministries; Chuck Colson of Watergate fame is a noted example. Some are more restricted than others, depending on circumstances, age, and education (e.g., illiterate new believers will be severely handicapped), but God still has a perfect will for them. He is an all-wise God, who fashions His will to our circumstances. But His will seems to begin at conversion.

One biblical principle impacts on this: "To whom much is given, from him much will be required" (Luke 12:48 NKJV). The Lord demands more of a believer who has fifty years left to serve Him than one with five years. Both can do God's perfect will for the remainder of their lives *if* they walk in unbroken fellowship with Him and are obedient in all things.

▷ *I broke every moral law of God before I was saved. Can I still do the perfect will of God?*

Absolutely! The gospel is "good news" because God doesn't hold us accountable for anything we've done before conversion. That's the mystery of God's grace. His forgiveness is total. His perfect will for you, however, will depend on your age and the life-molding decisions you've made to that point. If, for example, you are a mother of four small children and are married to an unsaved husband, His perfect will for you will commence where you are. Doubtless it will include becoming the most godly wife and nurturing mother you can be. If you are a college professor, business professional, or laborer, His perfect will may directly relate to your present vocation. If He leads you away from it, you can expect His guidance to be gradual, one step at a time. Remember, God never directs us to do anything He will not enable us to accomplish.

If, however, you are a drug pusher, prostitute, or porno publisher, you can expect an immediate change of vocation! That type of activity is clearly outside God's moral will for your life.

Our dear friends Jim and Lenora Woodall, missionaries to the Nicaraguan refugees living in Costa Rica, lived 180° in opposition to God's revealed will until their conversion. Though God had spared Jim's life in Vietnam as a marine, not until he and Lenora married did Jim come to faith in Christ, after both were over thirty years old. Immediately they began studying God's Word and applying it. After seven years of spiritual growth, they felt led of God to work with refugees in Costa Rica. If you could see their work and the way God is blessing them, you'd agree that at this point, they're doing God's perfect will for their lives.

But as I write these words en route home from a week in Costa Rica, delivering clothes and humanitarian aid to thousands of refugees, many of whom have just fled their country because of the Communist regime, I'm reminded that missionaries aren't the only ones who can have that experience. While in Miami, typing the first draft of this chapter into my computer, I was interrupted by a very successful Christian businessman friend from San Diego. I've known this man and his wife for many years. They, too, are enjoying God's perfect will, using God's principles in their business and personal lives.

▷ *If God fully forgives Christians who repudiate His will, why do they have to settle for God's good or acceptable will after they repent?*

This will occur only if they've made some life-molding decisions during the period of carnality and rebellion. Suppose a Christian man repents of a past that included drug use and subsequent loss of an arm in an accident while using drugs. God will forgive him and welcome the prodigal back into the household of faith, but He will not restore his arm. If the man had been an athlete, writer, builder, or architect, you can see how it might never be possible for him to return to God's perfect will. Forgiveness, yes, but from then on he must settle for God's acceptable or good will. In addition, if a Christian leader's sin has ruined his or her testimony, it may take time for that person to return to God's will. Forgiveness is instant. Restoration to service usually takes time—and sometimes a person's service can never be restored.

▷ *Is it possible for others to cause me to miss God's perfect will?*

That's a tough one! I'm inclined to think so, particularly for a married person. Your spouse may resist God's call on your life. Usually, however, God will change the person's mind in time for you to conform to His will.

On the other hand, I know two great Bible teachers whose wives fought them in every phase of their spiritual occupation. One wife even stood up in the front row at a Bible conference and humiliated her husband; while under the influence of alcohol, she called him a "hypocrite" and a "phony." The other leader was given no Christian support in the raising of their children, none of whom followed their father's faith. It's difficult to judge whether these women kept their godly husbands from doing more than God's acceptable will. That's for Him to reveal at the Judgment.

▷ *Is it possible to miss the will of God altogether, if a person repents on his or her death bed?*

Only God knows, of course, but the Bible teaches that there is a sin unto death that, if committed, can cause a person to lose his or her life prematurely (1 John 5:16). Consequently, the person will reach heaven but will have lost all rewards when he or she gets there. Part of God's will for every Christian is that we "lay up for [ourselves] treasures in heaven" (Matt. 6:20a). We can't do that unless we are submitted to God's will.

Summary

God has a perfect will for the life of every believer until we sin or neglect His will long enough to miss it. Then God wants us to repent and seek to do His acceptable will. If we persist in our sin and rebellion long enough, we may so entangle our lives that we'll have to settle for God's good will.

To avoid that problem, fill your mind with God's Word daily, walk in the Spirit, and seek His leading in all the important decisions of life. But if you "blow it" and then come to your senses—recognize that you're living outside His will, stop whatever you're doing, get on your knees immediately, and recommit your life to God's perfect will. Begin once more to subject all your decisions to Him, His Word, and His Spirit (more on this process of restoration in chapter 13).

The best way to keep from missing God's perfect

will is never to make any selfishly motivated major decisions while disobeying His moral or universal laws. Admittedly, that's difficult for most of us to do during a long Christian life. That's why Paul challenged us to walk in the Spirit and not in the flesh. The second best way to keep from missing God's perfect will is to keep short accounts with God. Daily Bible reading and prayer should be as regular as eating physical food and getting exercise. That enables His Spirit to reveal any mistakes you may be making before they cause serious damage. The longer Christians walk in their own way, making their own self-directed choices, the more apt they are to follow decisions that will cause permanent damage to their lives.

⑥

The Bible: Your Road Map for Living

We've explored the various decisions we make in our lives, and we've examined what we already know about God's will. Now let's move toward learning some practical steps to discovering God's will for our individual lives.

We Need Direction

No one would think of driving across the country without a detailed road map. Yet many people travel the road of life with little more than the guidelines observed in their parents and other models. No wonder they wander off on so many detours!

God has given us a sixty-six-volume road map that provides not only guidelines and principles enabling us to make correct choices in life but also examples of real-life people—some who obeyed those guidelines and succeeded; others who rejected them and failed. The Bible is "a lamp to [our] feet and a light for [our] path" (Ps. 119:105). On a dark night, however, the best flashlight in the world is worthless if you can't find it or don't know how to use it.

God has given us the Scriptures to help us make thousands of decisions as we travel the increasingly complex road of life. Unfortunately, most Christians today seem rather ignorant of the Bible's relevance, so they base most of their decisions on human reasoning. They fail to see that knowing God's Word is one of the most important prerequisites to finding His will. God is a God of principle, and He has written these principles in His Word. The more thoroughly we know those principles, the easier it will be to make life's decisions.

Two Kinds of Wisdom

Two kinds of wisdom prevail today: "the wisdom of God" (1 Cor. 1:18–30) and "the wisdom of this age" (secular humanism). The wisdom of this age is also called "the wisdom of the world," "the wisdom of the wise," or "human wisdom." Frankly, the wisdom of this age is rather impressive stuff. Our minds are inundated with it in secular education, from kindergarten through graduate school. It dominates the media and determines most public policy today.

Unfortunately, most Christians seem to know more about human wisdom than God's wisdom. That may result from a lack of opportunity to hear, read, study, and memorize the Word of God. Some Christians, of course, are mentally too lazy to spend time filling their minds with the Word of God so that when they make decisions, they can draw on divine wisdom instead of this world's philosophy.

Happy is the Christian who understands that human wisdom is limited, unscriptural—and wrong. Admittedly, it may seem very attractive, but if we contemplate a major decision and muse inwardly, "It seems right to me," we'll be wrong every time—at least in finding God's will for our lives.*

Write this down on the frontal lobe of your brain: by nature we don't think God's thoughts. Paul warned the people of his day, "The natural man does not receive the things of the Spirit of God, . . . nor can he know them, because they are spiritually discerned" (1 Cor. 2:14 NKJV).

When you became a Christian, you were not freed from your old sin nature. Instead, God added to your nature a spiritual side that must enlighten and direct you if you wish to make right judgments. Still, even one's immature spiritual nature is not a sufficient guide. It must be saturated with the Word of God, which your new inner nature will receive as a message from Him. From this point on, decision making on all levels becomes a lifetime practice of discovering God's will according to His Word and obeying it.

Everyone Wants Happiness

God is interested in your happiness. He didn't save you to make you miserable for the rest of your life. The Bible repeatedly begins its promises with "Happy is the man . . ." or "Happy is he that . . ." Read the Psalms and Proverbs, underlining the references to "happy"— or "blessed," as the older versions translate the word.

Happiness should not be confused with some exotic or sexual experience. Admittedly, many *sensual*

---

*Tim LaHaye, *The Battle for the Mind* (Old Tappan: Revell, 1980), a synopsis from Chapters 3 and 4.

experiences can produce a sensational kind of happiness—for a short period of time. That's not the kind of happiness God is interested in. He desires your maximum, long-term happiness—a happiness that results in a deep sense of blessing.

But how is happiness obtained? By obedience to the Word of God. The psalmist declared, "Happy are those whose lives are faultless, who live according to the law of the LORD. Happy are those who follow his commands, who obey him with all their heart" (Ps. 119:1–2 TEV). Our Lord Himself said, "How happy are those who hear the word of God and obey it!" (Luke 11:28 TEV).

As a Christian counselor, I've learned long ago why people become unhappy. Even before I heard their stories, I knew they were disobeying one or more of God's principles. My responsibility was to help them discover which principles they were violating and how they could change their conduct to conform to God's will. Those who refused to obey His Word prolonged their misery.

Two Kinds of Roads

As we proceed down life's journey, we can choose between two roads: the road of this world's wisdom and the road of God's wisdom. The first leads us through deserts, wastelands, and jagged mountains of perplexity and frustration. By contrast, the wisdom of God takes us through the *oasis* of understanding and the valley of delight, leading us confidently to fulfillment in this life and the blessings of eternity, which Christ has prepared for us in heaven. Though all Christians will eventually be ushered into heaven, many will have endured futile or miserable lives because they didn't know or follow biblical principles on a daily basis and because they placed so little value on the Bible when reaching significant decisions.

We must be aware that the road of this world's wisdom will try to lure us—through daily newspapers, magazines, public education, and the nightly news. Unless we purposely fill our minds with God's wisdom, we'll find ourselves walking down the road of this world's wisdom. We need to remind ourselves repeatedly that by human nature our ways are not God's ways and that "there is a way that seems right to man, but in the end it leads to death [or failure]" (Prov. 14:12). As Dr. Francis Schaeffer cautioned, "All roads from humanism (man's wisdom) lead to chaos."

The Bible: God's Road Map

To find our way along the road of God's wisdom, we need a map. That map, of course, is the Bible, God's inerrant directions for finding His will. So if you are serious about finding His will, become equally serious about learning His mind as revealed to us in the Holy Scriptures. Read the Bible daily, immersing yourself in His wisdom.

Remember the story in chapter 1 about Alison, the pregnant, single parent who was on the verge of having an abortion? When she finally decided to look to God's Word for direction, she found His will. She realized she was on a downward spiral of sin, and she finally decided to cancel her appointment to have an abortion. After she decided not to get the abortion, she continued to find strength from God's promises found in Psalm 37, especially verses 3–5 and 23. She hung on to those promises during the difficult days of living with the consequences of her adultery. God's road map led her off the road of the world's wisdom and back on to the road of God's wisdom.

A well-trained, high-tech engineer was offered a substantial pay increase to come work for a major competitor. He recognized that it wasn't his skill they sought but the inside information he'd learned as a faithful employee. The wisdom of this world, of course, merely labels such activity the "brain drain." But the engineer wasn't interested in following the world's wisdom. Instead, he consulted the road map, the Bible. There he discovered that taking the job would lead him down the road of dishonesty and cause him to violate the eighth commandment, "You shall not steal" (Exod. 20:15). As a result of consulting the map, he rejected the offer. The principle of honesty undergirded his decision, and within a short time he realized that he had acted correctly.

In finding God's will, nothing is more critical than the road map of His Word. If you refuse to consult it, you'll wander from the road of His wisdom. If you consult and follow it, you'll forge ahead with assurance and joy down the highway of His will.

Avoid the Hunt-and-Peck System

Some Christians try to substitute the daily reading of Scripture with what I call the "hunt-and-peck system" as they seek God's will. They respect the Word enough to read it when searching for His will, but they open it at random, expecting God to give them specific revelations for life's major decisions. Frankly, this usually leads to hopeless confusion.

Senator William Armstrong, the dedicated Christian who unashamedly lets his love for our Lord permeate his political career, related a humorous story at this year's annual prayer breakfast in Washington. A businessman, using the hunt-and-peck system in discerning God's will, opened the Bible at random and put his finger under the word "wheat." That inspired him to buy a farm and plant wheat, which became a very successful venture. The next time he used that method, his finger came to rest on the word "oil." So he bought land in Texas and drilled an oil well, which at first became profitable. But when the bottom dropped out of the oil industry, he again turned to the Bible for guidance, and this time his undirected finger came to rest on the words "Chapter 11"! Obviously, that was the last directive he wanted to read.

Had that man regularly read God's road map for living, filling his mind with God's fundamental thoughts and principles, he could have used the road signs covered in the next chapter to reach wise decisions. Instead, his haphazard use of the Scripture led to his ruin.

Know the Word and Do It

When God chose Joshua to be Israel's leader, He gave him the classic key to success—a key that has served as a model for thousands of Christians:

> "Do not let this Book of the Law depart from your mouth; meditate on it day and night, so that you may be careful to do everything written in it. Then you will be prosperous and successful. Have I not commanded you? Be strong and courageous. Do not be terrified; do not be discouraged, for the LORD your God will be with you wherever you go" (Josh. 1:8–9).

As we've already noted, the key to success is *knowing* and *doing* God's Word. Naturally, action (doing His will) must be preceded by knowledge (discovering His will).

Discover God's Wisdom

The following passages describe the importance of learning *God's wisdom* for decision making:

> "I, wisdom, dwell together with prudence;
>> I possess knowledge and discretion.
> To fear the LORD is to hate evil;
>> I hate pride and arrogance,
>> evil behavior and perverse speech.
> Counsel and sound judgment are mine;
>> I have understanding and power.
> By me kings reign
>> and rulers make laws that are just;
> by me princes govern,
>> and all nobles who rule on earth.
> I love those who love me,
>> and those who seek me find me.
> With me are riches and honor,
>> enduring wealth and prosperity.
> My fruit is better than fine gold;
>> what I yield surpasses choice silver.
> I walk in the way of righteousness,
>> along the paths of justice,
> bestowing wealth on those who love me
>> and making their treasuries full.
>
> "Now then, my sons, listen to me;
>> blessed are those who keep my ways.
> Listen to my instruction and be wise;
>> do not ignore it.
> Blessed is the man who listens to me,
>> watching daily at my doors,
>> waiting at my doorway.
> For whoever finds me finds life

and receives favor from the LORD."
(Prov. 8:12–21, 32–35)

In this ancient book filled with the wisdom of God, Solomon, the wisest man who ever lived, shared the wisdom God gave him directly as well as the wisdom he had gleaned from his father, David. Solomon and David conferred on us more of God's principles for living than any other Old Testament writers.

> When I was a boy in my father's house,
>> still tender, and an only child of my mother,
> he taught me and said,
>> "Lay hold of my words with all your heart;
>> keep my commands and you will live.
> Get wisdom, get understanding;
>> do not forget my words or swerve from them.
> Do not forsake wisdom, and she will protect you;
>> love her, and she will watch over you.
> Wisdom is supreme; therefore get wisdom.
>> Though it cost all you have, get understanding.
> Esteem her, and she will exalt you;
>> embrace her, and she will honor you.
> She will set a garland of grace on your head
>> and present you with a crown of splendor."
> Listen, my son, accept what I say,
>> and the years of your life will be many.
> I guide you in the way of wisdom
>> and lead you along straight paths.
> When you walk, your steps will not be hampered;
>> when you run, you will not stumble.
> Hold on to instruction, do not let it go;
>> guard it well, for it is your life.
>> (Prov. 4:3–13)

There is no easy way to learn the wisdom of God. It's a strenuous, painstaking, demanding task. But if you want to become a wise Christian who makes the proper life choices, you'll have to schedule part of your time each day for reading and studying the Bible. Job, a man of God who faced many perplexing decisions, stated, "I have treasured the words of His mouth more than my necessary food" (Job 23:12b NKJV). Studying God's Word is a matter of habit. Read the Bible every day for two months, and you'll develop Job's appetite for God's Word.

Paul rebuked the Corinthian church because since their conversion, they hadn't spent the necessary time feeding on the Word. Consequently, they had remained baby Christians.

> Brothers, I could not address you as spiritual but as worldly—mere infants in Christ. I gave you milk, not solid food, for you were not yet ready for it. Indeed, you are still not ready. You are still worldly. For since there is jealousy and quarreling among you, are you not worldly? Are you not acting like mere men? (1 Cor. 3:1–3).

What Is the Wisdom Literature?

While "all Scripture is given by inspiration of God, and is profitable" (2 Tim. 3:16a NKJV), you'll find that some passages are more valuable than others for making decisions. The historical books, Genesis through Esther, scatter much wisdom throughout their pages, but most of the text covers the history of God's dealing with the patriarchs and Israel.

The wisdom literature of the Old Testament is found in the Psalms, Proverbs, Job, Ecclesiastes, and the Song of Solomon. Since we are New Testament Christians, you may find even more help in certain New Testament passages, particularly those in James, 1 John, 1 and 2 Peter, Ephesians, Galatians, and Colossians. Add to that John 14–17 and Matthew 5–7, and you will have identified an effective body of God's wisdom without having to negotiate through the entire Bible before making important decisions.

Five Ways to Learn the Wisdom Scriptures

Acquiring the wisdom of God is not difficult, now that we have reduced the task from sixty-six to thirteen books, plus seven specific chapters in the Gospels. Consistently incorporate these passages into your daily life, just like eating three meals a day. A spiritual meal of from twenty to thirty minutes each day, over a period of time, will provide you with a solid understanding of God's wisdom. The following five ways are covered in detail in my book *How To Study the Bible for Yourself.** In it I provide charts and a guide that will in three years time give you a thorough working knowledge of God's entire Word. By the end of the first year, however, you should have enough of God's wisdom implanted in your mind to be able to make wise decisions.

The Navigators, a para-church ministry, has probably helped more people learn the Word of God than any other program I know. Their founder, the late Dawson Trotman, made famous the five methods of learning the Word of God. I have used these personally for years and have taught them to many men and women in small-group discipling Bible studies. Your regular use of these techniques will spiritually enrich your life and make discerning God's will much easier.

Hear the Word. "How happy are those who hear the word of God and obey it!" (Luke 11:28 TEV). Of all the methods of learning God's wisdom, the one most

*Tim LaHaye, *How to Study the Bible for Yourself* (Eugene, Oregon: Harvest House, 1976).

often used is "hearing." It's probably the way you first learned of your need to receive Him. Now that you are a member of His divine family, add to your "hearing" the following.

Read the Word. "Happy is the one who reads this book . . . and obey[s] what is written in [it]!" (Rev. 1:3a TEV). Reading is the foundation of all learning. Make it the pattern of your life to read God's Word daily.

Study the Word. "Study to show thyself approved unto God, a workman that needeth not to be ashamed, rightly dividing the word of truth" (2 Tim. 2:15 KJV). The difference between a strong, effective Christian and the weak person who stumbles down the highway of life is usually the degree to which the person truly studies the Word. One can learn almost any subject by regularly studying it. That is particularly true of God's Word.

Memorize the Word. "Your word I have hidden in my heart, that I might not sin against You" (Ps. 119:11 NKJV). Memorizing one verse of Scripture a week is not difficult for anyone who will consistently review the verses. Nothing will speed the learning process and help you safeguard your life from needless mistakes of judgment like memorizing God's Word.

Meditate on the Word. "Blessed is the man . . . [whose] delight is in the law of the LORD, and in His law he meditates day and night" (Ps. 1:1–2 NKJV). Meditation is all but a forgotten art today. It means *think!* Those who think over the concepts they've heard, read, studied, and memorized will be able to apply God's wisdom to the decisions they must make in life.

Summary

God always leads His children within the confines of the principles of His Word. And as we've already noted, one of His prime characteristics is consistency; consequently, He will never lead us to violate His Word. For instance, would God lead us to steal or kill or commit adultery? Never! That would be in violation of His character.

Yet many Christians make important decisions at a time when their deceitful hearts are pressuring them to put aside God's principles and follow the promptings of their hearts (or in some cases, their glands). Believe it or not, one young woman asked me to pray about whether or not she should marry her unsaved boyfriend. She was startled when I refused. When she asked me why I wouldn't pray with her, I told her, "Because the Bible forbids you to marry an unbeliever." Immediately I directed her to read 1 Corinthians 6:15–20 and 2 Corinthians 6:14–18 aloud. An auditory review of God's key principles made her decision quite obvious.

That decision was rather simple. But what about the story in chapter 1 of Becky, the pregnant girl who with her parents wanted to know if she should go ahead and marry the father of her unborn child—even though he was not a Christian? What is God's will in her situation? His Word says she should not be "unequally yoked" to an unbeliever. She found God's will in His Word. This is a question that almost all pastors face several times in their ministry, particularly during this permissive stage in history. Having sex with someone does not signify marriage, and even pregnancy doesn't change the fact that God wants Christians to marry only Christians. Becky needed considerable help in working out her problem and getting back into God's will for her life. Making another unscriptural decision (like marrying the unsaved father of her unborn child) wouldn't have corrected her unfortunate sexual decision.

In Becky's case, we found a Christian couple who

wanted desperately to adopt a child. Through a Christian attorney we worked out a plan that enabled her to be assured that her baby would be raised in a Christian home. The adoptive parents paid all the expenses, and Becky was able to pick up the pieces of her life—without the unsaved young man whose moral values were obviously a hindrance to her. Because of Becky's emotional involvement with the young man, it was necessary that I confront her with such Scriptures as 1 Corinthians 15:33 to convince her that he was the wrong person at the wrong time in her life.

7

Eight Road Signs
for Decision Making

God not only gives us a clear road map to direct us to His will, but He also gives us signs that further guide us and confirm His direction in our lives. Have you ever thought about what it would be like to travel across the country without road signs? "Speed limit 55," "Los Angeles, 25 miles," "Divided highway ahead," "Merge," "Road construction next 20 miles," "Deer crossing," "One way"—these signs give us information that is more specific than the information on our maps. Without these signs, we would move ahead somewhat blindly, unable to chart accurately where we need to go. Road signs help confirm we're on the right road or warn us that we're on the wrong one. They warn us of upcoming dangers or situations in which we'll need to be especially alert.

If we obey these signs, we'll end up at the right place—in God's will. If we ignore them and follow our urges or human wisdom, we'll end up in chaos. By following these road signs, we can be assured of making the right choices at key points in our lives, which will help us find God's will and reduce life's confusions.

God gives us eight basic road signs that point us to His will. A sensitive response to each will assure us of a safe, confident journey down the road of God's wisdom.

Road Sign 1: Surrender

The first sign that directs you to God's will is your ability to surrender to His Word. You must determine in advance that you'll obey God's will—even before you know what it is. We've already seen that God has a will for your life. But when you discover it, will you do it— even if it's something that at first you don't really find appealing? In His model prayer for Christians, our Lord taught us to pray, "Your kingdom come, your will be done on earth as it is in heaven" (Matt. 6:10). That is still the model for the child of God: do on this earth the will of God, as it is fulfilled in heaven.

The apostle Paul's example of surrender is worth looking at. The key to the apostle's greatness is found in his conversion prayer, "So he, trembling and astonished, said, 'Lord, what do you want me to do?'" (Acts 9:6a NKJV). As a good Jew, Paul had enough Old Testament understanding to recognize that God had a will for his life. As soon as he discovered that the God he was seeking was none other than the Lord Jesus Christ, he immediately surrendered his will to Him. As long as Paul lived that surrender, he made right life choices.

King David reflected that same basic attitude for most of his life. In Acts 13:22, God said of him, "I have found David . . . a man after My own heart, who will do *all* My will" (NKJV, emphasis added). That is understood in David's prayer, "Open my eyes, that I may see wondrous things from Your law" (Ps. 119:18 NKJV). That should ever be our attitude as we approach God's Word: "Reveal to me out of your Word what you want me to do, and I will be glad to do it." This is unreserved surrender to God's will in advance. Christians who willingly surrender themselves in advance will gain sufficient biblical guidance to make decisions quite easily.

Many Christians, I fear, are not surrendered to God's will before they identify it; therefore, they find it difficult to get direction from God. They tend to pray, "Dear Lord, show me Your will for my life, and if I like it, I'll do it." While such thinking is common, it's definitely wrong. You may be asking, "How can I tell if I'm *really* surrendered to doing God's will in advance?" Very simply. Are you already following His instructions? For example, do you attend church regularly, in compliance with God's command not to forsake "the assembling of [yourselves] together," referring to the Lord's day of worship (Heb. 10:25 NKJV)? Does the world and its attractions have a powerful grip on your life, causing you to follow it instead of Christ? We are told, "Do not love the world or the things in the world. If anyone loves the world, the love of the Father is not in him" (1 John 2:15 NKJV). What about tithing, soul winning, and prayer? If you aren't doing what you already know to be God's will, it's unlikely that you are surrendered in advance to His purposes for your life.

Our Lord should be a prime example in such cases.

He said, "My food is to do the will of Him who sent Me" and "I have come down from heaven, not to do My own will, but the will of Him who sent Me" (John 4:34a; 6:38 NKJV). Ask yourself, "What do I really want out of life?" Do you insist on having your own way? Or do you love and trust God to the point that you want to embrace His will more than anything else?

Whether or not you realize it, your conversion made Him *Lord* of your life: The Bible says, "Whoever calls upon the name of the LORD shall be saved" (Rom. 10:13 NKJV). Now keep Him Lord by following His instructions implicitly.

At times God's directives are easy to accept; at other times we respond by faith—if we are surrendered in advance. Paul must have had this in mind when he wrote, "I beseech you therefore, brethren, by the mercies of God, that you present your bodies a living sacrifice, holy, acceptable to God, which is your reasonable service" (Rom. 12:1 NKJV). Your life and mine, now that we are Christians, should be living sacrifices to the will of God. Note that Paul bases that challenge on God's mercies. We can trust a merciful God to promote our best interests in the long run, even though in the short run we may be dubious. Long-range happiness results only from doing His will.

Remember Ron, the printer mentioned in chapter 1? He too learned the value of surrendering his will to the commands of Scripture. If you remember the story, Ron had wanted to expand his company by merging with another businessman who would turn over his part of the business in five years. The arrangement that had initially looked good to Ron slowly began bothering him. Before he signed the final papers, he came to ask some advice. I asked Ron if the other businessman was a Christian. When I found out he wasn't a believer, I pointed Ron to 2 Corinthians 6:14–18, particularly the command not to be "unequally yoked together with unbelievers" (NKJV), which in this case included a non-Christian business partner.

Ron's response was one of complete surrender to the road map. He immediately said, "Then I won't do it." He broke off the negotiations with the businessman and watched another man become this businessman's partner. Ron learned later that the first businessman had already mortgaged his equipment to the hilt ($42,000) and then left town—machines, shop, and a hefty bank loan. Ron realized that by surrendering to God's road map, he had saved himself $42,000 and a probable bankruptcy.

Road Sign 2: Prayer

A second road sign that leads you to God's will is prayer. The Bible challenges us: "Ask, and it will be given to you; seek, and you will find; knock, and it will be opened to you" (Matt. 7:7 NKJV). The apostle Paul added, "Be anxious for nothing, but in everything by prayer and supplication, with thanksgiving, *let your requests be made known to God*" (Phil. 4:6 NKJV, emphasis added). To the Colossians he declared, "For this reason, since the day we heard about you, we have not stopped praying for you and asking God to fill you with the knowledge of his will through all spiritual wisdom and understanding. And we pray this in order that you may live a life worthy of the Lord and may please him in every way: bearing fruit in every good work, growing in the knowledge of God" (Col. 1:9–10).

These are only three Scripture verses that verify that God wants us to pray when seeking His direction. He wants us, of course, to pray about everything and to "pray without ceasing" (1 Thess. 5:17 NKJV).

Personally, I've found that prayer is usually a Christian's first resort when he or she considers God's will. They may not pray about minor decisions such as deciding which of three routes to take across town, but when they're told their child's life is in danger, their first reflex is to pray. My wife and I have been there. When doctors told us there was little likelihood our daughter would live through the night unless we chose the best of three possible treatments, very honestly, we were too overcome to make the choice by ourselves. We went to a quiet place and prayed before making the decision. We asked God to guide our thoughts, knowing that He promises to do that when we ask. The choice was easy because God led us to the same decision— today Lori is the mother of three children.

Some people use an elaborate procedure when they pray. By contrast, I start by confessing my sin so nothing interferes with the process of prayer. Then I make my specific request known to God and thank Him for His goodness and presence in my life. This method may sound simple, but I suspect it approximates the way most Christians pray. Note the simplicity in this incredible promise: "If you then, being evil, know how to give good gifts to your children, how much more will your Father who is in heaven give good things *to those who ask Him!*" (Matt. 7:11 NKJV, emphasis added).

Prayer is an integral part in helping us to make proper choices. But God has something else in mind in teaching us to pray when seeking His leading. He wants us to draw closer to Him, to acknowledge Him in all our ways.

God seems to have four ways to get our attention so that we earnestly seek Him:

1. Financial difficulties
2. Health problems—personal or family
3. Marital disharmony
4. Uncertainty about a change in life

Such difficulties should draw us closer to God and enrich our spiritual life. As a result, the decision-making trauma that drives us to pray will prove beneficial.

Road Sign 3: The Holy Spirit

The third road sign that points us to the will of God is the indwelling Holy Spirit. Chapter 3 has already explored the importance of being filled with the Spirit. Now we want to look at the Spirit's guiding force in our lives. When we are controlled by the Spirit, His presence within us directs us to God's will. Our Lord promised, "The Spirit of truth . . . dwells with you and will be in you. . . . *He will teach you all things, and bring to your remembrance all things that I said to you*" (John 14:17, 26 NKJV, emphasis added).

Passages from Romans 8 help us to understand how the Spirit leads us in our lives, decisions, desires, and happenings—even when we aren't aware of it.

For those who live according to the flesh set their minds on the things of the flesh, but those who live according to the Spirit, the things of the Spirit. For to be carnally minded is death, but to be spiritually minded is life and peace. Because the carnal mind is enmity against God; for it is not subject to the law of God, nor indeed can it be. So then, those who are in the flesh cannot please God. But you are not in the flesh but in the Spirit, if indeed the Spirit of God dwells in you. Now if anyone does not have the Spirit of Christ, he is not His. And if Christ is in you, the body is dead because of sin, but the Spirit is life because of righteousness. But if the Spirit of Him who raised Jesus from the dead dwells in you, He who raised Christ from the dead will also give life to your mortal bodies through His Spirit who dwells in you. Therefore, brethren, we are debtors—not to the flesh, to live according to the flesh. For if you live according to the flesh you will die; but if by the Spirit you put to death the deeds of the body, you will live. For as many as are led by the Spirit of God, these are sons of God (Rom. 8:5–14 NKJV).

Likewise the Spirit also helps in our weaknesses. For we do not know what we should pray for as we ought, but the Spirit Himself makes intercession for us with groanings which cannot be uttered. Now He who searches the hearts knows what the mind of the Spirit is, because He makes intercession for the saints according to the will of God. And we know that all things work together for good to those who love God, to those who are the called according to His purpose. For whom He foreknew, He also predestined to be conformed to the image of His Son, that He might be the firstborn among many brethren (Rom. 8:26–29 NKJV).

The child of God should develop a sensitivity to the inward leading of the Holy Spirit. Learn to pray inwardly about everything.

One night as I was leaving Chicago's O'Hare airport, I had to decide whether I would take my scheduled flight—which was late—or a flight that would get me home thirty minutes earlier. After silently praying, I decided to take the scheduled flight, which by this late hour was almost empty. An engineer bound for my hometown settled in next to me and asked, "What do you do?" When I told him I was a minister, I thought he would jump off the plane! But within twenty minutes he turned to me again. "Explain something to me. My brother-in-law has been telling me that he has been 'born again.' You are a theologian. What does he mean?" Long before we reached our destination, this engineer prayed to receive Christ. Thank God I read the road sign of that "still, small voice" that caused me to select the slowest way home.

That is what the Word means when it says, "He shall direct your paths" or "[He] will guide you with [His] eye" (Prov. 3:6b; Ps. 32:8b NKJV). He "nudges" our spirit or "impresses" our spirit or "broadens" our heart. Such inclinations are usually the Holy Spirit within.

D. L. Moody used to say something to this effect: When you get a "burden" to do something that doesn't violate the Scriptures, it is the will of God.

The Spirit's guidance will always coincide with God's Word. The Holy Spirit wrote the Word, inspiring His servants to transcribe it. Therefore we can be certain that He will not lead us in ways that are contrary to it. In many instances He brings Scripture to mind just when we need it in making decisions.

Road Sign 4: Circumstances

When you speed down the freeway, you not only read the official road signs but you also pay attention to the traffic signs. If it's rush hour, you begin to concentrate more intensely on the traffic signs.

So it is in life. You pay attention to the circumstances that are evidences of divine providence. These circumstances or signs take many forms, and Christians must learn to be sensitive to them. They may involve job transfers, financial difficulties, national or international problems (such as military service), sickness, or even the death of a loved one.

Circumstances have a profound effect on everyone—particularly a Christian whose loving heavenly Father works *all things* "together for good to those who love God, to those who are the called according to His purpose" (Rom. 8:28 NKJV).

George Washington, possibly the greatest man in American history, was a believer in divine providence. He certainly had seen God work through circumstances at Valley Forge and many other places during the Revolutionary War. Washington saw God grant his small, inexperienced army victory over a much larger professional force. My research on the book *The Faith of Our Founding Fathers* verified that twenty-seven personal letters written by our first president carried a consistent message: "Had it not been for the strong hand of providence, our cause would have been lost."

Circumstances also have led many of us to our life's mate. In my case, I enrolled in a college I didn't want to attend—as a result of God's providence (and my mother's prayers). The third week of school I found myself in the dining hall, seated next to a pretty young woman named Beverly. Discovering that we "just happened" to be from the same city, we walked out of that dining hall talking—and have been walking and talking together ever since. Later in life we discovered all kinds of reasons why neither of us should've been at that precise spot at that specific time. "Circumstances" had brought us together.

But our story is not unique. Millions of Christians have found their life's companions that way. Conversely, many Christians at a time of disobedience found themselves in a place they never should've been (because it was so obviously forbidden in Scripture), met some stranger, and married out of the will of God, missing God's perfect will for their lives.

Have you ever wondered why preachers so often use the selection of a mate as an example of finding or missing God's will? There are two reasons. One, few decisions in life have a more profound effect on a person's life, and two, it is scriptural. How Isaac found Rebekah is one of Scripture's exciting stories of seeking and finding God's chosen mate. Remember the story? Abraham asked his servant Eliezer to go to his relatives to find a bride for his son Isaac. As Eliezer approached the city of Nahor, he asked the Lord to send to the well a young virgin who would offer him a drink and then provide water for his camels. When Eliezer finished his prayer, he looked up and saw Rebekah, a young woman who was from Abraham's family and who met all the requirements (Gen. 24). Could that be coincidence? Hardly! From such experiences someone was moved to say, "God always gives His best to those who leave the choice to Him."

Open Doors

Another common circumstance sign is an "open door." Recently a school teacher friend began to lose interest in the teaching job he'd held for twelve years. As he prayed about God's leading, an open-door offer came in the mail, providing a school position in another part of the country, near his aged parents. His entire family was thrilled with the prospects—and I wouldn't be surprised to learn that his parents' health will soon require his physical presence. In this case, the open door of opportunity matched the desire of his heart.

Such open doors are scriptural. Our Lord said to His faithful children, "I have set before you an open door, and no one can shut it" (Rev. 3:8b NKJV). Some think this promise was given only to ministers and missionaries, but the text is not limited to the professional Christian worker. It was given to the whole church of Philadelphia, a prophetic foreglimpse of the entire Bible-believing church of our day, numbering into the millions.

The apostle Paul's much-celebrated vision, calling him to Macedonia to help open Europe to the gospel, was a singular experience in his life. At times he referred to the "open door" or "door of utterance" that God had placed before him. For example, "And pray for us, too, that God may open a door for our message, so that we may proclaim the mystery of Christ" (Col. 4:3). Actually, the term "open door" really means an obvious opportunity to serve God. But remember, God can close doors as well. Don't immediately assume, however, that a closed door means that such an opportunity is permanently denied to you. Perhaps the timing is off. If the burden to do something persists, if it's not contrary to the Word of God, and if you have submitted it to the

Holy Spirit, keep looking—the door may open at a later date.

Two years before God called Bev and me to leave our church in Minneapolis and move to San Diego, He gave me a burden to minister in California. A church interviewed me, but it was already involved in calling someone else. For two years that burden persisted, particularly during those winters when it was 36° below zero! And then, right out of the blue, as the result of a "chance" meeting with another minister, I was recommended to the Open Door in San Diego, which became my parish for twenty-five wonderful and fruitful years.

Remember, what God has done for others, He wants to do for you. Keep your eyes open for the open-door opportunities in your life—but don't neglect the other signs either. Particularly check those circumstances that seem like God's leading in accord with His Word. If God is directing, neither the Holy Spirit nor life's circumstances will ever lead you to violate His Word. The most obvious example is a young woman who tried to convince me that she had met Mr. Right on a business trip. "He just happened to take the seat next to mine and just happened to be staying in the same hotel." She went on to explain that he made her "tingle" as no one ever had before. Just one thing was wrong: he wasn't a Christian. According to the Bible, our final authority, Mr. Right immediately became Mr. Wrong.

Road Sign 5: Peace in Your Heart

The fifth road sign that points us to God's will is a peaceful heart. God is not the author of confusion. Scripture tells us that "the wisdom that is from above is first pure, then peaceable" (James 3:17a NKJV). When God is leading you in some specific way, you can expect His supernatural peace that you are doing His will. Scripture tells us that we not only can determine God's will but also can enjoy His confidence when we find it (see 1 John 5:14–15 NKJV). The confidence John identifies seems equivalent to the peace Paul cites when he tells the Philippians not to worry but to pray with thanksgiving about the burdens and decisions of life. As a result, "the peace of God which surpasses all understanding, will guard your hearts and minds through Christ Jesus" (Phil. 4:7 NKJV). Notice that both your mind and heart will be given peace when you discover God's will.

A person whose heart and mind are not at peace will endure a time of inner turmoil, indicating either that God is not leading or that this isn't the right time. When I showed the woman mentioned previously that marriage to Mr. Wrong was not God's will, she experienced inner conflict. But I would rather see her suffer temporary anguish than foul up her life or have to settle for less than God's perfect will. When she closed that wrong door and opened her eyes to find God's true leading, she at least had peace.

Let's look again at the story in chapter 1 of Ted, the Navy captain who needed to decide whether to accept the open door to become a rich test pilot (and quite possibly a dead one) or to stay in the Navy and trust God for his advancement. Ted left my office looking for the peace of God, committing the final decision to Him. After a period of waiting, gradually the peace to remain in military service and rely on God for the future caused Ted to sign up for another tour of duty. Shortly after that, he was ordered to take command of a Navy air base for two years—the only requirement he needed before he would be eligible to be promoted to admiral. Ted may become an admiral someday, but in the meantime, he and his wife are serving the Lord and their country while enjoying God's peace.

I've found that peace functions like an "umpire" when making decisions. The bigger the decision, the more peace God seems to administer. Perhaps that explains why, when I'm asked to sign someone's Bible, I always add, "Let the peace of God *rule* in your hearts" (Col. 3:15a NKJV, emphasis added). The word *rule* literally means "umpire." In an athletic contest the umpire decides whether the runner is "safe" or "out," "in bounds" or "out of bounds." Inner peace is God's supernatural sign that decides "safe" or "out" as we attempt to discern His will.

Is God Interested in Your Car?

Buying a car on a minister's salary when I had five mouths to feed was a traumatic experience. We wanted a Mercury station wagon, but we couldn't afford a new one. I had bought and sold used cars while in college, so I was certain that I could find one with plenty of miles left in it. While reading the used car ads, I spotted a special clearance with a twenty-four-hour return clause. We went to the dealer and picked out a car that looked impressive. We examined it carefully for defects (worn mats and brake pedal, scratched paint, bald tires) and felt that we'd made a good selection.

We took our new possession home and formally dedicated the car during our evening devotions. The next morning, however, I awakened with a troubled spirit and for some unexplained reason found myself looking at the want ads again. That morning a dealer was advertising a car one year older—which I really didn't want because it reflected the old body style—but somehow I found myself driving across town to look at it. Out of thirteen salespeople, the one who waited on me walked to the car we had just purchased and remarked, "Where did you get that car? You didn't buy it, did you?" Then he explained that he recognized the car. It had belonged to his next-door neighbor, a traveling executive who "had driven it over 90,000 miles—much of it pulling a trailer!" That was definitely not what we needed! We later learned that the dealer from whom we had bought the first car had a standard policy of turning all odometers back.

We returned the first car within the twenty-four-hour time limit and a few days later bought one with only 6,000 miles on it. It served us faithfully for seven years. When we dedicated that car, we thanked God not only for the accompanying peace but also for giving us unrest about the wrong vehicle.

It's wise never to make major decisions unless the umpire, the Holy Spirit-inspired peace of God that surpasses all understanding, calls the decision "safe!"

Road Sign 6: Your Own Desires

A sixth road sign that will help you find God's will is your own desires. It is difficult for some Christians to believe that doing God's will can mean pursuing their own interests. We forget that God's Holy Spirit is within us; when we are surrendered to His will, He can give us godly desires. Romans 8:16 indicates that the Holy Spirit "bears witness with our spirit that we are children of God" (NKJV). According to Romans 8:14, "For as many as are led by the Spirit of God, these are sons of God"

(NKJV). One evidence that we are supernaturally indwelt by the Spirit is that we are led by God.

Paul told the Philippians, "It is God who works in you both to *will* and to *do* for His good pleasure" (Phil. 2:13 NKJV, emphasis added). Similarly, the psalmist taught that if you "delight yourself in the LORD . . . he will give you the desires of your heart" (Ps. 37:4).

One well-known Bible teacher has stated that when Bible-taught Christians are committed to God's will, doing what they wish to do is fulfilling His will. I would carry this concept a step further. Don't be surprised if the first indication of God's will for you is your desire to do it. You may not identify it as a "burden from the Lord" or a "witness of the Spirit," but that's exactly what it is. If a decision is biblically legitimate, it's probably God's will—as long as it doesn't violate your peace of heart. We have to remember that we are dealing with a loving heavenly Father who delights in making our joy *full* (John 15:11 NKJV). What a miserable life it would be if God were to call us to activities we despised! Personally I don't think that would happen. Admittedly, we may initially shrink from God's calling, for we may not be walking in the Spirit, and a carnal heart doesn't respond readily to God's will. But as we yield again to His urging, a positive response will gradually appear.

For a Spirit-filled believer, doing God's will is usually a matter of fulfilling the desires of our heart—so long as we are surrendered to His Word and His will. If for some reason your desire doesn't coincide with God's will, just surrender yourself to Him and He will engraft that desire until it conforms to His will. In most cases what a Spirit-filled Christian wants to do most in life is really the will of God for his life.

Road Sign 7: Godly Advice

Another significant road sign is the advice God sends our way in the form of dedicated Christian counselors. This is particularly true of major decisions in life. Most decisions can be made on our own, but the more important and complex the decision, the more deliberate we should be in evaluating the issues. At that point, the Lord may send us someone in whom we can confide, someone who can objectively administer good, sound, Bible-based advice.

During the early part of a football game, you may observe the quarterback making his own decisions, though the coach may give some directions via an incoming player. But when the score is tied and it's third down and three yards to go on the thirty-yard line, the quarterback almost invariably calls a time-out and trots over to the coach and other field generals for a high-level huddle. The decision is too big for one person to make. There are just too many options to choose from.

Life is like that. You can make ordinary plays on your own as you walk in the Spirit. But when the game's outcome depends on a single judgment or when your life and those you love may be affected for years to come by a momentous decision, you need all the help you can get.

The Husband Who Didn't Tell

Let's look again at the story from chapter 1 of Dick, the Amway salesman who wondered whether or not he should tell his wife about his adultery. He needed scriptural help in making his decision. When I asked him how he thought his wife would accept his confession, he replied, "It would kill her!" That, of course, was a gross exaggeration. It would, however, break her heart and cause her enormous (and, in my opinion, unnecessary) grief. Since he had genuinely repented, was taking all the right steps never to repeat the sin, and had shared it with me as his pastor, I advised him to do five things:

1. Do a Bible study on sin. Explore the consequences of sin as well as God's forgiveness of the sinner.

2. Accept God's forgiveness by faith and put the experience behind him as Paul said, "Forgetting those things which are behind" (Phil. 3:13b NKJV).

3. Thank God for His forgiveness (1 John 1:9), for his wife, for their love and future together; and ask God to protect his wife from unnecessary hurt. Each time he remembered his sin, he was to thank God for His forgiveness.

4. Love his wife as husbands are commanded four times in Scripture (Eph. 5:25–33; Col. 3:19).

5. Be sensitive to the Holy Spirit. If it was God's will for him to confess it all to her, the Spirit of God would make that clear.

At this writing, twelve years later, he reports they have a beautiful marriage, and she still hasn't had to go through the heartache of knowing about his sin.

Advice to the Wife of a Porno Freak

Another example is the story from chapter 1 of Nancy, the wife who discovered her husband's addiction to pornography. She was wise to seek godly advice. She was torn by her desire to be a submissive wife and yet not to give in to her husband's increasing demands to do what she felt was unnatural and demeaning, particularly since her past experience proved that whenever she gave in to her husband's specific demands, he would soon tire of that and come up with some other evil idea found in his perverted pornographic magazines.

Taking her back to Scripture where sex is always put in the context of love, I showed Nancy that Hebrews 13:4 didn't endorse everything two people do in bed. The Greek word *bed* is *kotay,* which we translate "coitus" or "sexual intercourse." I compared that with Ephesians 5 and other passages that command that husbands love their wives as they do their own bodies. After reading that Scripture passage and others like 2 Corinthians 10:5, Nancy could understand how her husband's thoughts should be abandoned and brought into obedience to Christ.

After we prayed together, Nancy went home and explained to her husband that she would submit to him for the act of marriage, but she would never again submit to those degrading acts he wanted her to perform. He was so obsessed by his perverted passions that he rejected the love of a real woman for his weird fantasies—and he divorced her. At the present time Nancy is making a home for their two children, while enjoying peace in her heart that she's done the right thing. Her husband still refuses to get spiritual help and turn his will over to Christ. And like many porn addicts he still feasts on that depraved material. The last chapter of this story has not yet been written.

Advice from Others

The counsel you receive is as good as the person who gives it. If you want godly advice, you must consult godly people. Solomon reminds us, "Where there is no counsel, the people fall; but in the multitude of counselors there is safety" (Prov. 11:14 NKJV). Godly counselors tend to offer similar advice—because they study the same book.

At some point in your life, however, you may need to get advice from a non-Christian—perhaps in the medical/health, accounting, or legal professions, where a specialist is required and where no Christian in your community may be qualified to advise you. An ophthalmologist counseled my mother to have laser surgery on her eye. At her age that was a heavy decision, and she couldn't find a Christian specialist for professional confirmation. When she called to ask my counsel, I advised her to go to her Christian family doctor and ask her opinion of the specialist's advice. The conference caused my mother to proceed with the treatment that extended her vision for several years. If you need technical advice from an unbeliever, listen to the advice—just don't make his or her opinion your final decision.

Some believers are too proud to seek advice. One Christian leader I know made a disastrous decision that all but cost him his ministry. When asked why he didn't go to someone else for help, he replied, "Who does my counselor go to for advice?" In other words, no one on earth was wise enough to advise him. If he had been more humble and if he had looked for direction from a godly source, he and the church of Jesus Christ could have been saved much heartache and disgrace.

Actually, I've found in Washington, D.C., where certain leaders make decisions that affect the lives of millions of people, that many leaders are humble enough to seek the advice of others. Take the example mentioned in chapter 1 of my friend Stan, the congressman who needed to decide whether to run for the U.S. Senate or to remain in the Congress. Several days after Stan and I talked about his decision, I phoned him and told him I'd been praying for him. I went on to suggest frankly (though tactfully) that he was on a suicide mission. If he left Congress, we would lose not only his valuable services but also his Christian witness in that important body. He thanked me for that "discouraging word" and a few days later announced his change of mind and returned to the Congress. I'm not implying that my call alone changed his mind, for as it turned out, several of his friends voiced similar concerns. But he heeded our advice, and today he's still serving God and his country as a conservative Christian voice in Congress because he dropped out of an ill-timed Senate race.

You're never too big to accept the aid of those who are spiritually qualified. Solomon charged, "For by wise counsel you will wage your own war, and in a multitude of counselors there is safety" (Prov. 24:6 NKJV). He likewise affirmed, "Ointment and perfume delight the heart, and the sweetness of a man's friend does so by *hearty counsel*" (Prov. 27:9 NKJV, emphasis added).

Scripture gives many illustrations of people seeking advice. Moses, of course, set a pattern by going to Jethro, his father-in-law, for counsel. Paul instructed older women under Pastor Titus's care to be counselors to the younger women. Almost all of Paul's epistles, particularly in the last few chapters, are punctuated with practical advice about how to live and how to make decisions.

One of my seminary professors, Dr. Grant Howard, gives very practical advice in his excellent book *Knowing God's Will and Doing It.*

> God puts a lot of coaches along the sidelines for us during our life here on earth. The believer ought to recognize when the fourth-and-one situations are present and take time out, go to the sidelines, and talk to a coach. It may be your mom, dad, pastor, youth minister, teacher, sponsor, or just a close friend whom you respect. But be careful—go to the right sidelines! Get your counsel and advice from those on your team. And when you get to your sidelines, go to the coach, not to the water boy or the fourth-string tackle who has played only seven minutes all season. As for time-outs—they are unlimited. Call one whenever you need one. One other point: Go while the game is still in progress. For example, a man who knows things are not going well in his marriage but is convinced he can handle it by himself may discover that when he finally goes to the sidelines for help, the game is over and it is too late. Time has run out.*

Beware of Incompetent Advisers

The Christian must be careful at this juncture to seek the counsel of godly people. Remember the admonition of the psalmist, "Blessed is the man who walks not in *the counsel of the ungodly*" (Ps. 1:1a NKJV, emphasis added). That first verse in the Psalms introduces a salient principle. It can be dangerous to receive

---

*J. Grant Howard, "Counsel and the Will of God," *Knowing God's Will and Doing It!* (Grand Rapids: Zondervan, 1976), 64.

counsel from unsaved people who don't use the Bible as their manual on human behavior. They will almost always render advice based on human wisdom, and that can be 180° in opposition to God's will for you. Scripture teaches that "the natural man does not receive the things of the Spirit of God . . . nor can he know them" (1 Cor. 2:14 NKJV). Don't expect intelligent, concerned, unsaved people to impart godly wisdom—they don't understand the Bible.

Another word of caution is essential. Be wary of ill-conceived advice from carnal Christians or veteran Christians who allow personal ego to destroy their objectivity. In such cases, ask the Holy Spirit to give you adequate warning and to direct your feelings and thoughts toward a proper solution.

When I was twenty-four years old, fresh out of college and in my first church, I led the music at a summer camp where the speaker was a world-renowned Bible teacher—with an ego to match his reputation. When he heard the name of the Christian school I had just graduated from, he was incensed. "The first thing you have to understand is that you do not have an education, young man!" He then prescribed this remedy: "Forget the training you have, go to the University of Minnesota and get a *real* education." Somehow in my youth that didn't seem to make sense. Four years in a Christian liberal arts university was to be discarded for a purely secular education in preparation for the ministry? That would be rejecting God's wisdom for human wisdom. So I ignored his advice and instead proceeded to seminary. Years passed, and I had an opportunity to relate that story to the president of my alma mater when it conferred on me an honorary degree. Once I identified the year of that outburst, the college president recalled rejecting that well-known preacher's offer to deliver a series of lectures to the student body—just six weeks before the preacher had given me his advice. So much for objectivity!

It was relatively easy to spot the error of that advice, even as young as I was, for it violated Psalm 1:1. The minister was claiming that a humanistic education (which was then rampant at the University of Minnesota) was more to be desired than biblically based training. Unfortunately, millions of Christian young people still heed that advice.

COMMON SENSE

Road Sign 8: Common Sense

The final road sign that leads us to finding God's will is common sense. Dawson Trotman used to say, "God gave you a lot of leading when He gave you a brain!" You may find his advice surprising. But the longer you read the Bible, the more your mind will guide you to make spiritual decisions. You, of course, make many more everyday or minor decisions than major, life-molding decisions. If you regularly read God's Word, these everyday decisions will be programmed by your God-guided mind almost subconsciously. We call that common sense.

When the Bible uses the term "sound mind," it means "common sense," "sober-minded," or "reasonable" (2 Tim. 1:7 NKJV). Bishops and deacons were required to have sound minds (1 Tim. 3:2; Titus 2:2 NKJV). Several passages teach that in the light of the coming of our Lord, we ought to live "sensibly" (1 Peter 4:7; Titus 2:11–12 NKJV). These texts clearly challenge us to use common sense in daily life.

God has given human beings amazingly complex brains, with the ability to think, reason, and learn from past experience. We have the capacity to develop common sense, particularly when we add to our own mental maturity the discernment we gain in regularly studying the Bible. God expects us to develop that common sense and to use it in making the most of life's decisions. It's our common sense that enables us to read the road signs mentioned above and make intelligent decisions in the light of our own circumstances.

The late A. W. Tozer, a gifted Christian leader, wrote a much-quoted tract entitled "How the Lord Leads." In it Tozer advises:

> Except for those things that are specifically commanded or forbidden, it is God's will that we be free to exercise our own intelligent choice. The shepherd will lead the sheep, but he does not wish to decide which tuft of grass the sheep shall nibble each moment of the day. In almost everything touching our common life on earth, God is pleased when we are pleased. He wills that we be free as birds to soar and sing our Maker's praise without anxiety. God's choice for us may not be one but any one of a score of possible choices. The man or woman who is wholly and joyously surrendered to Christ cannot make a wrong choice. Any choice will be the right one.
>
> But what about those rare times when a great deal is at stake, we can discover no clear scriptural instruction and yet are forced to choose between two possible courses? In such a situation we have God's faithful promise to guide us aright. Here, for instance, are two passages from the Word of the

Lord: "If any of you lack wisdom, let him ask of God, that giveth to all men liberally, and upbraideth not; and it shall be given him. But let him ask in faith, nothing wavering" (James 1:5, 6 KJV). "Thus saith the Lord, thy Redeemer, the Holy One of Israel; I am the Lord thy God which teacheth thee to profit, which leadeth thee by the way that thou shouldest go" (Isa. 48:17 KJV).

Take your problem to the Lord. Remind Him of these promises. Then get up and do what looks best to you. Either choice will be right. God will not permit you to make a mistake.*

What If God's Direction Doesn't Seem to Make Sense?

Obviously A. W. Tozer, who had counseled hundreds to find God's will for their lives, believed in using common sense when we are walking in the Spirit. But at rare times in our lives God may ask us to do something that doesn't make common sense. In such situations expect Him to make His will extremely clear by greater use of the other road signs. For example, it didn't make common sense for Noah to spend 120 years of his life building a huge sea-going vessel when it had never rained before. And it wasn't common sense that compelled Philip to leave a city-wide evangelistic crusade to witness to a lone Ethiopian in the desert. Nor was it sensible for Joshua to march around the city of Jericho seven times or for General Naaman to dip seven times in the Jordan River. But in each of these situations, God gave special insight or revelation to match the unusual instructions.

Such experiences are not limited to biblical charac-

---

*A. W. Tozer, "How the Lord Leads," a tract available from Christian Publications of Harrisburg, Pennsylvania.

ters. The pastor of a booming church in North Dallas, Texas, experienced just such a leading from God. While pastoring a growing congregation of over 700 people, he was invited to teach a Bible class in the home of some people who had moved to North Dallas, a newly developing area. After a few months, 35 people prayerfully asked him to pastor their new flock full time, which meant he'd have to leave his established church.

The situation didn't make sense. Even the denomination's church-growth committee, after studying the North Dallas area, had concluded that the community didn't possess the ingredients to build a new church. After much prayer and soul searching, the young pastor went to the eight-acre piece of property the new church was hoping to buy, where he earnestly sought God's direction. The Holy Spirit met him in a special way that afternoon and communicated to his spirit that he should accept the new pastorate. So he resigned his established church and accepted responsibility for that handful of people, approximately one hundred the first official Sunday. Today, ten years later, the congregation numbers ten thousand members and has close to six thousand people attend Sunday school and church on a given Sunday. It's considered the fastest-growing church in the history of the denomination—which is known for its strong evangelistic ministry and super churches.

As a rule of thumb, you can expect a special indication from God when He asks you to do something that flies in the face of common sense. Most people only confront such momentous decisions once or at best a very few times in life. Most of your decisions, even in these complex times, will make common sense to a believer (they probably won't make sense to an unbeliever!). Why would the pastor of a beautiful, growing, established church leave it to tackle a dream without a tangible building? Why would a Christian pre-med student feel led to leave medical school and go to seminary to study for the ministry? These decisions will rarely make sense to the nonbeliever. "It's a waste of talent," most would protest. But if God makes His will unmistakably clear, you had better do it!

Summary

Finding God's will in the haze of this crazy, mixed-up world of ours is like landing an airplane in the fog. As a pilot, I've often left the sunny sky above ten thousand feet to make an approach through the fog to my home airport. From a relaxed state of mind, I suddenly become very alert to everything on my instrument panel.

One of the pilot's biggest dangers in landing an airplane is becoming fixated on one or two instruments. Making a safe landing depends on constantly reading *all* his instruments. Long before I descend into the fog, I check my maps, the altitude, my airspeed indicator, and the distance-measuring device so that I know exactly how far I am from the field. Then I check the direction finders, V.O.R.s, and the glide slope in an attempt to stay within fifty feet of my assigned altitude and descent rate. I'm in constant touch with the unseen radar control operator, and I constantly check my M.D.A.—the minimum descent altitude on the field. Then I watch for the landing lights to line up at the end of the runway. I know I'm on the glide slope properly when the three red lights merge into one and when the marker beacon ignites a light on the instrument panel.

So it is in finding God's will for our lives. We must look at *all* the road signs that point to God's will. We can't just look at the circumstances or the witness of the Holy Spirit or the counsel of our friends or the peace of God or even our common sense. But when the road signs begin to line up in a straight line, we know we're properly approaching the "runway" to God's will. It's a matter of coordination. When we coordinate the signs for finding God's will, we'll find that all the signs merge into one, clearly pointing to His will.

Since you are unable to see the future, you must trust the signs, just as an instrument pilot relies on the plane's instruments. Even when instincts dictate a contrary response, trust your instruments—in this case your ability to surrender, your prayers, the Holy Spirit, circumstances, the peace in your heart, your own desires, godly advice, and your common sense. It may take time to wait until all the signs are lined up and you receive "clearance," but in the long run it will save you an enormous amount of time—and unnecessary grief.

8

Don't Make
Snap Decisions

We often make poor decisions because we make them too quickly. We want to know God's will *now*, but He may have other things in mind for us. He may have some lessons He wants us to learn. As we've already seen, we spend more time in fellowship with God when we're earnestly trying to find His will. And those are learning and maturing times for us. Making us wait on Him is one way He tests and strengthens our faith.

Besides, we can almost never go wrong when we wait on the Lord. Too often we rush impetuously into a decision before we know what God has in store for us. As the British theologian J. I. Packer reminds us, " 'Wait on the LORD' is a constant refrain in the Psalms. It is a necessary word, for God often keeps us waiting. He is not in such a hurry as we are, and it is not His way to give more light on the future than we need for action in the present or to guide us more than one step at a time.

When in doubt, do nothing, but continue to wait on God. When action is needed, light will come."*

I have only one real fear in this world: getting out of God's will in a major area of life. I haven't always made correct decisions, especially when working under duress. I particularly remember one snap decision I made on a public platform in Washington, D.C., before television cameras. It was a wretched decision that took me three or four years to live down. Looking back, I realize that I should've prayed about it and used the road signs. As a general rule, we can agree with the maxim, "Haste makes waste!"

The biblical advice "In all your ways acknowledge Him, and He shall direct your paths" (Prov. 3:6 NKJV) implies that a time factor is involved. Little time is needed for small decisions, but you should take extra time with the big ones. In addition, I recommend that for the major, life-changing determinations, you should savor the decision at length and allow God time either to confirm or negate it.

The Hardest Decision I've Ever Made

As noted earlier, the most significant decision I've made as a pastor was resigning from a wonderful church after twenty-five years of service. I had watched that church grow from 3 employees to 337, including all the faculty in the ten-school Christian educational system, Christian Heritage College, and several other ministries. As the senior pastor and leader to some degree of all these entities, my decision was going to affect hundreds of other people.

---

*J. I. Packer, *Finding God's Will* (Downers Grove: InterVarsity Press, 1985).

It became apparent to me that I could no longer burn the candle at both ends—holding thirty Family Life Seminars a year, pastoring a growing church that met in three locations, writing one book a year, actively trying to warn Americans of the dangers of the not-so-subtle religion of secular humanism, and trying to mobilize the body of Christ to become more active in the political process. My candle was getting rather short. Speaking engagements were opening to me all over the country, and I felt guilty that I was neglecting my congregation. Our growth rate dropped from 10 percent a year to 3 percent. While I had a very capable staff of eleven associate pastors, I had tried over a four-year period to find a key man who would come and co-pastor the church with me, providing the congregation with a full-time shepherd, but to no avail.

The first step for me came on December 31, as my wife was driving us to Los Angeles for a Christian New Year's Eve party. Rousing from my study, I turned to her and said, "Bev, I believe God wants me to resign our church."

I'll never forget her response, "Well, it's about time!" I was flabbergasted by her reply. I had really expected her to say something like, "Oh, you can't do that!" Instead, she said, "I've known for over a year and a half that you would have to come to this decision."

"Why didn't you mention it?" I prodded.

She replied, "Because I didn't want to influence you. This has to be your decision. I don't want you ever to blame me if you feel that you have left the will of God."

That was an unusual response from her because we usually discuss all of life's issues freely. But she wisely maintained silence, feeling that I should initiate this major decision that was drastically to change both of our lives.

Waiting on the Lord

We earnestly prayed about the decision, studied the Word, talked to godly friends, examined the circumstances, and objectively tried to scrutinize the desires of our hearts. As the conviction settled on both of us, we knew that, as difficult as it would be, God's will would be served by shifting ministries.

Then we did two things that we can recommend as you seek your heavenly Father's direction—particularly with regard to a major life decision. First, we began asking God, on the basis of 1 John 5:14–15, not only whether our move was His perfect will for our lives but that He would also give us the *confidence* that we were doing His will. Second, we began to *savor* the decision by giving God ample time to intercept us in case our decision was not His will.

Let me explain how those two steps worked in our process of coming to know His will. After we asked God to give us *confidence* in the decision we felt He was asking us to make, we felt that confidence grow. Every road sign lined up, and His peace umpired the decision. I even specifically asked God to give me such assurance that no matter what happened in the future, He would never let me second-guess the rightness of that decision. After six years, I've not doubted a single time that it was His perfect will. To be honest, I do miss being a pastor, and I could happily return to such a position if God so led. But in spite of the changes in my life and the church I left, I've never doubted the correctness of that decision.

As we *savored* the decision, we gave God time to correct us if we were somehow on the wrong track. In our case, our church's annual business meeting, at which I would need to announce my decision to leave, didn't occur for twenty-seven days, giving us almost a month to listen further to God. During each of those days we prayed for God's direction. If it wasn't His will for us to resign, we wanted Him to stop us in our tracks. And as we put out several fleeces, asking for tangible indications from God, each one came up wet, just as we had prayed.

When January 27, the day of the annual meeting, arrived, I was in full possession of the peace that passes all understanding. That didn't lessen the difficulty of announcing the decision, which took the entire church totally by surprise. However, subsequent events have proved without a doubt that it was the right decision.

I desire that same peace for you! But it will not come unless you give God time as you *savor* your decision. Then you can simultaneously fulfill God's will and enjoy the *confidence* that you are in the center of His will. This confidence rarely comes when we hurry or demand an instantaneous response. But if you wait on the Lord and have courage, "He shall strengthen your heart" (Ps. 27:14 NKJV). If you rush ahead into what you hope is God's will, you'll lack the confidence you could have enjoyed. The faith test that often accompanies a weighty step of faith greatly benefits from the assurance that although everything looks confusing and you don't fully understand God's dealings, you are nevertheless confident that His will is being perfected in you.

Bev and I first learned about the importance of that confidence when we left our Minnesota church and began our ministry in San Diego. Usually a new pastor's "honeymoon" stage continues for about a year. Ours lasted six weeks! We had no idea how divided the church was over two completely opposite Baptist associations. Most of the members were conservative in their theology, but some were loyalists to the liberal denominational fellowship. Both associations were wooing the congregation. Within six weeks I was perceived as favoring both the conservatives and the association they preferred. During the next three years the liberal loyalists did everything they could to get rid of me. Bev and I were sustained at the time by the confidence that although our ship was being tossed by gigantic waves, we were in the center God's will. As it turned out, we remained in that church twenty-five years and enjoyed some of our best experiences in the ministry. At times, then, that confidence will be the only source of your assurance and strength—and thus it's worth waiting for.

The confidence that comforted us after our decision to leave the Minnesota church and move to California was so reassuring that twenty-five years later, when we felt led to leave the California church, we coveted the same experience.

God Is Never in a Hurry

It took God six full days to accomplish the work of creation, which He could have completed just as well in an instant. He dealt with the first man, Adam, for 930 years. He instructed Noah to save humanity from the coming flood 120 years before He sent the rain. He promised Abraham a son who would introduce a new race of people into the world and then made him wait 25 years for the realization of that promise. He prophesied through Daniel that Israel's Messiah would be "cut off" (crucified); His people waited 483 years for the fulfillment (Dan. 9:24–26 NKJV). After He saved Saul of Tarsus, He took him to the desert to educate him for 3 years before using him in the ministry. Before our Lord ascended into heaven, He promised His church that He would come again for them—and we've been waiting almost 2000 years.

God is never in a hurry. We, however, usually are—and that is when we are vulnerable to make serious mistakes. When I'm in a rush to find His will, He reminds me of this cautionary verse: "For ye have need of patience, that, after ye have done the will of God, ye might receive the promise" (Heb. 10:36 KJV).

Patience! Sometimes it seems easier to do God's will than to wait patiently for Him to reveal it. Unfortunately, many Christians refuse to wait. They give a cursory look at their circumstances, check the desires of their heart, glance at one or two road signs, and then jump to a conclusion. That's why so many have fouled up their lives—and missed God's perfect plan.

Whereas "Hurry up!" seems to be the watchword of contemporary America, we need to have as our watchword "wait on the Lord." We need to learn that God is more interested in our knowing Him better—now—than in revealing His will to us—now.

9

The Double Check for Accuracy

All human beings possess a free will, which sharply distinguishes us from the animal kingdom. In His sovereignty, God chose to give every person full control over his or her own will. Thus we can accept the will of God or reject it; that's our choice.

The Bible is filled with stories of men and women who exercised their wills freely in response to divine directives. Many people rebelled against God, supplanting His will with their own: Cain, the first murderer; the people of Noah's day; the citizens of Sodom and Gomorrah; Pharaoh; Jezebel; and Judas Iscariot—to name a few. Some people consistently surrendered their wills to God's will: Enoch, Methuselah, Noah, Daniel, John the beloved disciple, and a few others. By far the majority of God's servants obeyed Him *most* of the time: Adam, Abraham, Moses, David, Peter, Paul, and others.

Self-Will or God's Will?

Many biblical characters committed themselves to doing God's will at certain times in their lives, but then they intentionally short-circuited His purposes with one or more acts of self-will. As a result, they suffered the serious consequences of failing to do God's will.

Take the apostle Paul for example. During most of his life, Paul surrendered his will to God, and was used by Him effectively. But Paul was an extremely strong-willed person by nature and temperament. At times he permitted his strong will to overrule God's will. Near the end of his third missionary journey (Acts 20), Paul apparently made up his mind that although God had called him as the special evangelist to the Gentiles, he would return to Jerusalem. He may have been home-sick; possibly he was hopeful of gaining approval of his peers for the incredible work he had accomplished; or he may have wanted to win some of his old Jewish colleagues to Christ. We can't be certain of his real motivation, but he was not led of the Spirit in that objective.

The Holy Spirit certainly revealed to Paul His will for the trip to Jerusalem. Acts 21 indicates that when he reached Tyre, the disciples through the Spirit warned him "not to go up to Jerusalem" (Acts 21:4 NKJV). But Paul steadfastly persisted. A few days later, after his company arrived at Caesarea, they stayed in the home of Philip, the evangelist. There a Judean prophet named Agabus, taking Paul's belt, bound his hands and feet and warned, "Thus says the Holy Spirit, 'So shall the Jews at Jerusalem bind the man who owns this belt, and deliver him into the hands of the Gentiles'" (Acts 21:11 NKJV). When the believers heard this, they "pleaded with him not to go up to Jerusalem" (Acts 21:12 NKJV). But Paul refused to listen. The Scripture tells us, "When he would not be persuaded, we ceased, saying, 'The will of the Lord be done'" (Acts 21:14 NKJV). Either all these disciples and prophets were wrong, or Paul was a hard-headed, self-willed person who had forgotten a significant principle: when spiritually motivated people recommend a change in direction, one had better seek the will of the Holy Spirit in the matter.

The ensuing experiences of the strong-willed apostle are well known. One sin usually leads to another, and we find Paul shaving his head and taking an Israelite vow in an attempt to please the Jews. He paid dearly for his brief period of self-will and spent two unnecessary years in a Caesarean jail for his trouble (Acts 22–26). He learned a valuable lesson from which all Christians may profit: God makes no mistakes in the directing of our lives when we submit implicitly to His will.

Although Scripture provides no comment, Paul must have confessed and been forgiven for this period of self-will, for we find that he again becomes very productive and usable in God's hands. The Lord doesn't carry a grudge, even when we sin. For He used Paul mightily in prison as a witness to governors, kings, and finally to Caesar himself. In fact, some of Paul's epistles were written *after* this display of flesh-dominated temperament. Reinstatement with God is an instant experience for any believer who acknowledges personal sin and yields himself or herself again to God—provided he or she has not committed a sin that disqualifies him or her for further service.

Although Paul responded and again became an effective servant, some believers refuse to recant their self-will, thus continuing to frustrate God in His attempts to lead them. Samson, for instance, repeatedly forfeited God's favor in his dealings with the Philistines. It was a blind, subjugated Samson who repented and gained the victory over his enemies—but at the expense of his own life. By contrast, David lived a godly life for fifty years, then failed miserably due to a series of self-willed decisions, including adultery, deceit, and murder. All of his iniquity was forgiven because he truly repented. And God didn't discard him as a servant. Nevertheless, the result of his sin and God's judgment certainly had an adverse effect on the rest of his life, limiting him severely. But in contrast to Samson, David wasn't destroyed by his self-will.

When God recalls you from the arena of self-will, don't let any time elapse between willful decisions and repentance. Then recommit yourself to God's will and let Him use what is left of your life.

Jesus and God's Will

Jesus Christ also wrestled with knowing and doing God's will. In the Garden of Gethsemane, Christ endured one of the most agonizing experiences in His life, evidenced by the fact that He sweat great drops of blood. Matthew's gospel tells us that Christ prayed three times for the will of God. In each case His prayers were identical: "O My Father, if this cup cannot pass away from Me unless I drink it, Your will be done" (Matt. 26:42 NKJV). Luke expresses our Lord's words this way: "Nevertheless not My will, but Yours, be done" (Luke 22:42 NKJV).

Whatever the contents of "the cup," our Lord didn't want to drink it. Some identify the cup as the crucifixion, but I reject that because His purpose was to die for the sins of the whole world. No, He wasn't resisting the weight of the Cross, for He said, "For this purpose I came to this hour" (John 12:27c NKJV). While no one can with certainty identify the contents of the cup, I tend to think it represents our sin. He was not afraid to die for our sins according to the Scriptures, even the excruciating and ignominious death by crucifixion. Rather, He objected to contaminating His holy nature by drinking of our sins. Yet He did it because that was the only means by which He could die as a substitute or sacrifice for our iniquity.

The significance of that cup is mirrored in Paul's appeal to the Corinthians to be redeemed to God through faith in Christ: "For He made Him who knew no sin to be sin for us, that we might become the righteousness of God in Him" (2 Cor. 5:21 NKJV). For the holy, sinless God-man, Christ Jesus, to become sin without committing sin, He had to partake of our sins innocently but deliberately. The contents of the cup, our sin, fills that requirement: God's will was for Him to be our substitute sacrifice.

The Double Check

But don't lose sight of the important fact that whatever the contents of the cup, our Lord gave us here a shining example of how to pray when seeking God's perfect will. Christ honestly stated *His* will—"Let this cup pass from me"—but subordinated His will to His Father's will by adding, "Nevertheless not My will, but Yours, be done." Our Lord's will was completely fulfilled in the will of the Father.

The same pattern is useful for us. When we face life's major crises, we can use the double check: honestly tell God what you believe is His will (or, in some cases, your will), but then pray "Nevertheless not my will, but Yours, be done."

I've shared this pattern with many people. In one instance, a dedicated young man told me all about the girl he identified as Miss Right. I asked him if he wanted this young woman as his wife more than he wanted God's will. He pondered that question for a moment and then replied, "Pastor, as much as I love her, I don't want her unless she is God's perfect will for my life."

So we knelt down in my office and prayed, "Dear Lord, as much as John loves Miss Right, if she isn't your perfect will for him, make it known to them. For more than they want each other, they desire Your perfect will." (Because I knew and loved the girl, too, I silently prayed that God would painlessly remove the love they felt for each other if that was to be His will.)

Within two months they both concluded they were not meant for each other. The decision was made without undue distress, and they remain friends to this day—both now married to other people and very happily serving the Lord.

The double check for God's will is both honest and direct. When you think you know God's will, tell Him your heart's desire, which hopefully coincides with His will. Then pray, "Nevertheless, Father, not my will, but Yours, be done." If you mean it, you will not rush ahead of God's program for your life. I've never met a person who honestly uttered that prayer and lived to regret it.

This was the advice I gave Joan, the "widow" mentioned in chapter 1. If you remember the story, Joan's husband, Charles, was missing in action in Vietnam and then later declared to be dead. Joan wanted to marry Bob, a Christian man from her church, but she had no assurance that Charles was really dead. The Air Force had officially notified her of the plane crash, but they had never discovered Charles' body.

What was she to do? First we checked the road map and the signs. Nothing in the Bible forbade her to marry Bob. She and Bob had prayed long and hard about the decision. Circumstances seemed to point to the rightness of marriage. But her peace wavered when she began to think of telling Charles' mother what she was thinking of doing. So we set a reasonable time period to savor the decision. She prayed, "Lord, you know I want to marry Bob; nevertheless not my will, but Yours, be done. If Charles is alive, please witness to my heart by lack of peace."

At the end of the suggested time period, her anxiety had left, and she felt the confidence she had prayed for. She and Bob were married. Three years later she received official notification that the crash site had been identified and that Charles' remains were being flown back to the United States. Because both Joan and Bob had carefully looked for God's leading, Charles' sons had a loving stepfather and two sisters to help them through the whole experience.

10

What About the "Fleece"?

Gideon, one of ancient Israel's judges, faced a major decision, probably the most important one he'd ever made. In the process he used a "fleece" to help him discern the will of God (Judges 6).

Gideon said to God, "If you will save Israel by my hand as you have promised—look, I will place a wool fleece on the threshing floor. If there is dew only on the fleece and all the ground is dry, then I will know that you will save Israel by my hand, as you said." And that is what happened. Gideon rose early the next day; he squeezed the fleece and wrung out the dew—a bowlful of water. Then Gideon said to God, "Do not be angry with me. Let me make just one more request. Allow me one more test with the fleece. This time make the fleece dry and the ground covered with dew." That night God did so. Only the fleece was dry; all the ground was covered with dew (Judg. 6:36–40).

What is a fleece? It's a specific request for some providential sign to confirm the leading of God. We find God giving providential signs other places in the Bible. We've already mentioned Abraham's servant, Eliezer, who found Rebekah, Isaac's wife-to-be (Gen. 24). In this case the sign was given as soon as Eliezer finished his prayer and looked up, for there she was—the virgin who fulfilled all that Eliezer had asked of God as an indication that this was indeed His specific leading.

Should We Use Fleeces?

Many Christians have found using a fleece a helpful method for reassuring themselves that they have indeed discovered God's will. On the other hand, some Christians reject this technique because, as they rightfully point out, we Christians have resources not available to Gideon. The Word of God can guide us, the indwelling Holy Spirit will lead us, and the godly counsel of pastors and other experienced believers may shed light in dark places. Gideon had none of those. But he did possess one significant advantage—God actually spoke to him audibly, as verified in such expressions as "Then the LORD said to Gideon."

Personally, I don't think God cares whether or not you use a fleece—just as long as it doesn't represent the only criterion used in discerning His will. Doubtless millions of Christians have found the will of God without ever using a fleece. On the other hand, many others find a fleece indispensable. I'm certain of one thing; no fleece will ever justify departing from the written Word of God. Whether God wets your fleece or wrings it out dry, His leading will conform to the principles in His Word.

Never forget that our heavenly Father loves us and

delights in leading us to do His will. We can't get into serious trouble by asking God to confirm His will in some way, particularly if we follow some simple guidelines. A sincere fleece seeker is usually neither resistant to God's will nor rebellious. The fleece seeker is merely trying to verify the divine program and is committed to doing it in advance, even before requesting the fleece. That certainly was true of Gideon. Somehow, I don't think he even had to fear that God might become angry just because he asked Him to dry the wet fleece and vice versa. God's wrath flashes only at those who hesitate in disbelief, delay unnecessarily, or rebel. He will never get angry at those who are simply uncertain that they are fulfilling His will.

A fleece shouldn't be used without careful deliberation, and by no means should it ever become the principal factor in deciding God's will. Let it serve as just one more weight of evidence that a specific action represents His will for your life.

Some Guidelines for Using a Fleece

Use a fleece sparingly. Never use the fleece technique for daily events. Walk in the Spirit and let Him guide you in making the routine decisions of life.

Use a fleece prayerfully. Only after much prayer and soul searching should a fleece be established. Note that Eliezer and Gideon didn't pick fleeces at random. Both were in prayer, communing with God, when they settled on the sign they asked for.

Save a fleece for major decisions, as the Spirit leads. You'll probably make no more than twenty major decisions during your entire life (marriage, vocational changes, education, etc.). Some of these choices can be made without a fleece. But when we are forced to make personal decisions that will affect the lives of others, which was the case with both Eliezer and Gideon, we sometimes will want to use a fleece.

Use a fleece to confirm God's will, not to find it. Long before reaching the fleece stage, you will have discerned the general leading of God through His Word, the Holy Spirit, peace in your heart, and the circumstances of life. Your fleece may help you select between one of two good possibilities, or it may help to confirm beyond doubt God's specific will in a matter.

Make your fleece specific. A fleece should never be ambiguous. It should establish a clear, uncommon sign that God can use to confirm His leading and to reveal Himself to you.

Personal Experience of Using a Fleece

My wife and I have used a fleece only three times in our lives: when we were married, when we left the Minnesota church, and when we left the California church. We have sought His will hundreds of other times, but those are the only circumstances during which we asked for a fleece.

In the case of the call to California, God's response to our fleece was so specific that we couldn't doubt His leading. I had preached two trial sermons on Sunday morning and evening and then had met with several boards and other people. The next day I flew home and shared the experience with Bev. I told her that the church's policy required that 90 percent of the congregation must vote for a person before the church would call him to be their pastor.

Wanting to know God's perfect will, we decided to use a fleece. We prayed and asked God for a specific sign: if we received 95 percent of the vote, we'd accept the call; if we received 94 percent or less, we'd continue to minister in our Minnesota church. (I didn't know until later that the church was so divided on everything that it took a miracle to reach a 90 percent agreement on anything!)

On Wednesday night after prayer meeting, George Hedlund, my dear friend and board chairman of our Minnesota church, came over to our home while his wife, Edna, was at choir practice. He was the only person in the church who suspected that my absence the previous Sunday was to candidate somewhere. I quickly reviewed the events of the weekend, including the fleece. When Edna joined us, the four of us prayed together for God's perfect leading. Then the phone rang. It was Harwood Murphy, the pulpit committee chairman of the California church, informing us that the San Diego church had extended us a call. He wanted to know my answer. When I nervously asked about the vote and figured out the percentage, it came to 97 percent! That was our answer! As the four of us cried and prayed, we recognized God's faithful and powerful leading in our lives.

Although our fleece prayer was not the only measure that we used in deciphering God's leading, it graphically confirmed what we already knew in our hearts: that the California church was God's perfect will for us.

If you opt for a fleece, use it sparingly, prayerfully, and specifically. Remember, your heavenly Father is more interested in helping you find His will than you are. And whenever you seriously seek God's will, you'll end up closer to Him and even more committed to doing His will.

11

Don't Flunk the Faith Test

Whenever you step out to obey God's will, expect a faith test. Most Christians conclude that stepping out on faith in obedience to the Holy Spirit's leading will propel them down a rose-strewn path. That's not the way it works. Most of the time it's like walking barefoot over a thorn-strewn path.

In Scripture, in what I have observed in others' lives, and in God's dealings with me, I've come to expect every step of faith to be followed by a rigorous test. That's one reason we need to be assured of God's will in the first place, for when that faith test arrives, we'll still enjoy the peace and confidence that we're doing His will.

Biblical Examples of the Faith Test

The Bible is filled with examples of godly people who experienced a faith test after they stepped out to

obey God's will. Abraham, one of the greatest men in
the Old Testament, was called to leave Ur of the
Chaldeans and go down into the land God promised to
him. God told him, "I will bless you and make your
name great. . . . To your descendants I will give this
land" (Gen. 12:2b, 7b NKJV). So what happened? Abraham obeyed God, took his family to what is now
Palestine, and set up an altar to worship the Lord.
Humanly speaking, one would expect God's blessing to
follow. Instead the passage continues, "Now there was a
famine in the land, and Abram went down to Egypt to
sojourn there, for the famine was severe in the land"
(Gen. 12:10 NKJV). This famine, which affected the
hundreds of people and livestock for which Abraham
was responsible, subjected Abraham to a faith test.
Could he trust God to supply his needs, or should he
take matters into his own hands?

Unfortunately, Abraham flunked God's first faith
test. In humiliation he was expelled from Egypt. Why?
Because he didn't turn to the Lord for further instructions. Like most of us, Abraham took matters into his
own hands. He went from living by faith to living by
sight—and thereby wandered from the path of God's
will.

The Israelites also were given faith tests. When
God led them out of Egypt, He promised to direct them
by a cloud in the sky during the day and a pillar of fire at
night. He delivered them from Pharaoh's army by
parting the Red Sea, allowing them to walk over on dry
ground. When Pharaoh tried to pursue them, he and his
army drowned. But the Israelites had no sooner crossed
the Red Sea than they were plunged into a whole series
of faith tests; from Pharaoh's armies to bitter water.

The New Testament provides similar experiences.
In Mark 4 and 6, just after the disciples had seen and

experienced miraculous events, they had their faith tested through dangerous storms that arose while they were in a boat. On both occasions the storms nearly sank their ship; only Christ's supernatural power saved them. When God called Paul to go over into Macedonia to preach the Gospel, he obeyed (Acts 16:10). Within a very short time he was thrown into a Philippian jail (Acts 16:23). The story ends, we remember, with the dramatic conversion of the Philippian jailer, but that didn't totally negate a distressing experience with an enraged mob, heartless magistrates, and an unjust imprisonment.

Expect Testing

Many Christians believe that if we're doing God's will, our lives will be trouble free. That is unscriptural. Testing after a deep faith experience is so common, both in the Bible and in life, that we should expect it. The writer of the psalms tells us, "Many are the afflictions of the righteous" (Ps. 34:19 NKJV). And in the New Testament, Jesus cautioned a scribe who had pledged his life to follow Christ: "Foxes have holes and birds of the air have nests, but the Son of Man has no place to lay his head" (Matt. 8:20). Obviously He wanted His followers to know that the life of a God-guided, Spirit-filled Christian will include suffering.

Testing has happened so many times in my life that when Bev and I felt led to move to Washington, D.C., and open offices there, I addressed the issue in prayer, hoping to avoid the test this time. I reminded the Lord that I had already started fourteen different organizations and that each one had been followed by a faith test. Since I had proven myself faithful, would He please waive the faith test this time? But He didn't! He enforced the principle outlined in James 1:3: "The testing of your faith produces perseverance."

Why Does God Test Our Faith?

So why does God test us? Evidently Christians who seek God's leading and then step out on faith need their faith tested. Obviously our heavenly Father knows we need the perseverance and patience that comes from such a faith test. Maybe we need to see God in our lives in a new way. God has promised to be with us and to see us through our trials, whatever they are—financial difficulties, health problems, family stresses, personal conflicts, or even attacks from Satan himself.

The apostle Peter also has indicated why God permits Christians to suffer or be tested: that "the God of all grace, . . . after you have suffered a while, [may] perfect, establish, strengthen, and settle you" (1 Peter 5:10 NKJV). The word *perfect* means "make mature." Part of our developmental process is made possible by suffering. Just as iron, to become steel, must be subjected to intense heat, so the Christian, to become mature, must submit to suffering—sometimes very intense suffering—whether we like it or not.

How Should We Respond to the Testing?

When you take the step of faith in obedience to God's will and shortly thereafter find yourself plunged into difficulties, don't despair. Reexamine your leading to make sure you weren't deceived in the process; if you are indeed in God's will, you'll experience God's peace that reassures your heart.

Times of testing are times to "count it all joy" (James 1:2 NKJV). Anticipate the strengthening of your faith and endurance, and remember that God promises to give wisdom to those who lack it (James 1:5). This chapter suggests that God provides special wisdom to His children when they endure periods of testing.

Accept trials as evidence that God has something planned for your future—something that requires additional strengthening. Following Jesus isn't easy. According to Christ Himself, "If anyone desires to come after Me, let him deny himself, and take up his cross daily, and follow Me" (Luke 9:23 NKJV) and "Whoever does not bear his cross and come after Me cannot be My disciple" (Luke 14:27 NKJV).

Adversity that arises after you step out on faith, then, doesn't indicate that God has stopped leading you or that you are no longer in His will. No, the Bible identifies it as a faith test. As Dr. Paul Little wrote, "We must avoid the mistake of thinking that we can be sure we are in the will of God if everything is moonlight and roses, if we have no problems or stress. Frequently, just when we take a step of obedience, the bottom falls out of everything. Then only the confidence that we are in the will of God keeps us going."* That's why it's worth extra time establishing that peace or confidence before taking the step of faith.

So keep on being obedient. Trust Him to supply your every need, and don't flunk His faith test!

▷ *And my God shall supply all your need according to His riches in glory by Christ Jesus (Phil. 4:19 NKJV).*

---

*Paul Little, *Affirming the Will of God* (Downers Grove: Inter-Varsity Press, 1971), 27.

12

Your Temperament's Influence on Finding God's Will

The most profound human influence on your life, whether you realize it or not, is your inherited temperament. Passed on by your parents through the genes at the time of conception, your temperament produces your spontaneous actions and reactions, affecting your likes and dislikes and even many of your prejudices. Your basic talents as well as weaknesses come from that temperament. In all probability, as much as 25–35 percent of your behavior is the result of the temperament you were born with.

Through the years, I've written four books on the subject and included one chapter on it in at least three others (see list at beginning of book). In addition, I've assisted my wife as she wrote two books on the subject: one about women and one about raising children. I've probably given over 600 lectures on the subject and have observed the effect of temperament while counseling thousands of people. I'm more convinced of its influence today than when I started studying it twenty-five years ago. In fact, I've noted its growing popularity in the secular world of motivation, management, industrial psychology, and sales training. Several temperament tests (or as some label them, personality tests) very similar to mine can help people determine their primary and secondary temperament, their strengths and weaknesses, and their vocational aptitudes. The LaHaye Temperament Analysis is the only one that describes how to overcome one's weaknesses by using spiritual resources. Already over 20,000 people have taken this analysis, and most of them have been very pleased with its results.

This is the first time, however, I've applied a person's temperament to the decision-making process of life—or the effect of a person's temperament on finding the will of God. Given the basic tools that God has supplied all of us with—God's Word (our road map) and such road signs as the Holy Spirit, circumstances, the counsel of others, etc.—people with different temperaments will process the same information differently. That doesn't mean they'll reach different conclusions because of temperament. Rather their temperaments will cause them to arrive at their conclusions differently. Some people reach decisions almost spontaneously; others agonize over every choice in life whether great or small, never quite certain they're selecting the best options. Both types of people can be very sincere, yet their temperaments make them approach the decision-making process in contrasting ways.

While leaving the full description of the four temperaments to my other books, I'll provide a brief description here.

The Four-Temperament Theory

The four-temperament theory is the oldest known theory of human behavior. Although the four were named and briefly delineated by Hippocrates about 400 years before Christ, Solomon described four kinds of people (Prov. 30:11–14) 500 years before that. Two hundred years after Christ, Dr. Galan, a Greek medical doctor, classified the four very carefully into ten strengths and corresponding weaknesses. His basic work has remained relatively unchanged through the centuries.

Today, however, since races and nationalities are so intertwined through mixed marriages, we find few people who fit entirely into one single category. Most people are a blend of two temperaments, one predominant and the other secondary. And while your secondary temperament will affect to some degree your decision-making process, your dominant temperament will influence the choices you make. Attempt to diagnose which of the following temperaments best describes you. Once you've made that determination, we'll examine that temperament's effects on your decisions. Keep in mind that the first two represent extroverts, the third and fourth introverts.

Meet the Sanguine Temperament

Sanguines are the most extroverted of all types; they could even be called super-extroverts. Sanguines are extremely talkative, outgoing, friendly, warm, humorous, and responsive. In fact, they hardly can look total strangers in the eye without responding to them in some way. Sanguines are fun-loving people who enjoy people and live a spontaneous life. Rarely worrying about the future or the past, they extract more pleasure out of today than do any of the other temperaments. Not usually deep thinkers, Sanguines interpret the events of life in the light of the immediate. At times they get into trouble because they rarely anticipate the results of their choices or actions. Their feelings play such a dominant role in everything that they're prone to make emotion-oriented decisions. As a rule of thumb, emotional decisions are almost invariably bad decisions.

Meet the Choleric Temperament

Cholerics are likewise extroverts, but they usually don't generate the decibel levels of the super-extrovert Sanguines. Cholerics are activists, crusaders, doers, pushers, and motivators of other people. Strong-willed, independent, and opinionated, Cholerics tend to be unyielding. Compromise is commonly difficult for them unless it serves their goal-oriented agenda. And they do have goals—for everything from physical fitness to child behavior. They are natural take-over types, who enjoy bossing other people around—whether or not the people like it. Cholerics try never to lose control of a situation, and they thrive on opposition. The most underdeveloped part of their nature is their emotions. Gaining their approval is almost impossible. Achieving goals is an all-consuming passion for Cholerics, and some gain the reputation of using people.

Meet the Melancholy Temperament

The most gifted of all the temperaments are the Melancholies—even though they are the last to appreciate their own gifts. Introverted by nature, they often have a high IQ and a deeply aesthetic nature, enabling them to appreciate the fine arts more than the other temperaments do. Melancholies tend to be moody and are easily discouraged. Born perfectionists, they often unnecessarily disparage themselves for not doing better, when in reality their productivity exceeds that of most other temperaments. They are self-sacrificing, serious, and fearful of failure. No one has a harder time with negativism and criticism (both at themselves and others). Conscientious by nature, they thrive on a worthy challenge or vision for investing their life but rarely can produce it by themselves. That's why so many Melancholies have found joy and fulfillment in dedicating their lives to Jesus Christ and the work of His kingdom. In my book *Transformed Temperaments*, I point out that God used more Melancholies in the Bible than all the other temperaments put together. They function best when dedicating themselves to a worthwhile objective greater than themselves. Christianity and its eternal perspective offers them that kind of lifetime challenge.

Meet the Phlegmatic Temperament

Phlegmatics are slow, calm, easy-going, super-quiet introverts. They never get upset, embarrass themselves by "running off at the mouth," or have to apologize for anything they've said. They rarely articulate ideas or feelings unless they are certain they won't offend or hurt another person. Phlegmatics are extremely nice people with pleasant, happy dispositions. Many are very funny because they possess a dry sense of humor. Natural-born diplomats and peacemakers, they are loved by children. They make pleasant, non-threatening friends—if it doesn't take too much effort to express camaraderie. Two of their chief weaknesses are fear and selfishness, though they manifest these traits so diplomatically that even some of their best friends don't recognize them. Although Phlegmatics are very competent by nature, their activity level is low. Indecisiveness and a tendency to remain a spectator may limit their growth and productivity.

Temperament and the Holy Spirit

My contribution to the field of temperament study has been in applying the Spirit-filled life to the various temperament blends. This has enabled many Christians to overcome their weaknesses through the ministry of the Spirit so that God can use their talents to the maximum. We don't have space in this book to cover that important aspect, but I suggest you review my other books on this subject. Through His Holy Spirit, God has provided enormous resources that enable you to become all that He has programmed you to be.

Actually, He is the best motivator of temperament and people. That's why I maintain that the two most important factors in our behavior are our inherited temperament and the motivation of the Holy Spirit. I've watched many undisciplined Sanguines, cruel Cholerics, morose Melancholies, and passive Phlegmatics become filled with the Holy Spirit and experience an incredible metamorphosis. The transformation was literally the result of God's power working on their weaknesses. Remember, you can't change your temperament. Like the color of your eyes, your IQ, your body size, and other genetically produced characteristics, your basic temperament will remain the same, for it is the result of your parents' genes at the time of conception. But the Holy Spirit will gradually overcome your weaknesses, enabling God to use the talents and abilities He has placed within you, the results of temperament strengths. And He will use you to the maximum—*if* you daily walk in the Spirit and *if* you identify and obey God's perfect will for your life.

Temperament Difficulties in Finding God's Will

Life is the net result of the choices you've made. If you've used the road map and the road signs described in this book instead of following your natural temperament tendencies, you are doubtless enjoying the luxury of operating within the perfect will of God right now. But if your major life choices have been made on the basis of your natural temperament, your life is probably fouled up. Or like many Christians, you may have followed a little of both—which means you are confronted with doing God's acceptable or good will.

The following analysis will show you the dangers of each temperament. Try to find your predominant temperament in this description.

Sanguines at Decision Time

Sanguines are extremely spontaneous people. In addition, they have sensitive emotions, making them cry easily, love hurriedly, and repent frequently. Their restless nature, causing them to rush headlong into things without weighing the consequences, is not conducive to making deliberate decisions. They respond to the first moving invitation, without evaluating what's involved.

As ministers, Sanguines do a good job of evangelism, and their new church will surge ahead for two or three years. Then they lose interest and quickly decide to move on to the next church. When doors open to them, they tend to speed through them without waiting on the Lord. That may explain why Sanguines usually move from church to church every three years.

As laypeople, Sanguines tend to repeat the same process—moving from job to job and city to city, continually disrupting the lives of their family. They mistake a natural restlessness for the leading of God. Often driven by intense ego, they may mistakenly see greater opportunities as divine calls.

Sanguines need to discipline themselves, particularly when making major decisions. They must avoid snap decisions, savor every carefully laid plan, and trust God. They need to learn not to rush into every decision, even if they feel that decision is God's will. They need to wait, trusting that God will keep the door open as long as it takes for them to become confident that the decision is the right one.

As we've seen, part of God's purpose in confronting us with decisions is to help us draw closer to Him and thus enrich our spiritual lives. Sanguines usually lack spiritual depth, not only because they are deficient in discipline but also because they rush into the decision-making process without adequately spending time with God to enrich their souls.

Sanguines are particularly vulnerable when making decisions of the heart because they are so emotional and feeling oriented. It's easy for them to follow the humanistic slogans: "If it feels good, do it" or "If it feels right, it must be right." But feelings can be deceptive. Many Sanguines wouldn't have married whom they did if they'd consulted God's road map and road signs instead of their heart.

Sanguines are "touchers," and this can get them into trouble in our sexually oriented culture. Although all temperaments have trouble with the flesh, Sanguines will violate their moral values more quickly than other types and then make decisions when they are estranged from God. All temperaments need to be very careful to walk in holiness during the decision-making process so they can follow God's leading rather than their glands. Sanguine decision makers should walk slowly during the decision-making process, spend extra time in prayer and Bible study, talk to friends, and wait for the peace that passes all understanding.

Sanguines have amazing potential for serving God if they wait on Him! If you are a Sanguine, learn self-control. Avoid that typical stampede into activities, generated by emotionally made decisions, thus limiting the use of your vessel by God. Listen to God's word to the psalmist, "Be still, and know that I am God" (Ps. 46:10). "Wait on the LORD; be of good courage, and He shall strengthen your heart" (Ps. 27:14 NKJV).

Cholerics at Decision Time

As soon as Cholerics become Christians, they face a difficult problem: learning to walk in obedience to God's road map, the Bible. Frankly, strong-willed Cholerics prefer self-reliance to submissive obedience. In the paraphrased words of the prophet, they need to learn to live not by Choleric might and not by Choleric power—but by God's Spirit.

Although Cholerics are practical and decisive by nature, they need to seek the Lord's leading instead of depending too much on their common sense. They tell me, "I call on God only for the big decisions of life, but I'm capable of making the routine choices by myself." Unfortunately, they interpret big decisions as whether the United States should withdraw from the United Nations or if this country should go to war with the enemy—courses of action in which they can contribute nothing directly. In other words, they rarely consult God for His leading regarding the direction of their own lives but lean on their own understanding.

Another difficulty relates to Cholerics' strong tendency to be independent and self-sufficient. Consequently they seldom ask the advice of friends. Having great confidence in their own ability to make proper choices, they rarely ask others who are in a position to be more objective.

When trouble arises, Cholerics tend to lower their heads and bulldoze their way through it. Consequently, instead of recognizing when they have made a mistake and changing course, they plow straight ahead, relying on brute force and durability rather than divine guidance. More than any other temperament, Cholerics will force the square peg into a round hole and then expect God to bless their success.

Unfortunately, Cholerics often enjoy working *for* God more than spending time *with* Him. They need to learn to "delight [themselves] in the LORD" (Ps. 37:4). But if Cholerics learn to submit their wills to God, He can use them powerfully. He can turn their goal-oriented drive into a useful tool for building His kingdom. When their wills are submitted to God, their tenacity and energy become positive forces.

Cholerics need to trust in the Lord, not in their own understanding. Like the Sanguines, they must use times of decision making to read and study the Bible, pray and seek God's leading, consciously surrendering their will to Him. Cholerics can accomplish great things for God *if* they will follow His plan instead of their own, recognizing the principle, "Except the LORD build the house, they labor in vain that build it" (Ps. 127:1a KJV).

Melancholies at Decision Time

The moment of decision—all decisions—is traumatic for Melancholies. They vacillate between accepting or rejecting, approving or censuring, agreeing or dissenting. Even when they proceed correctly, they rarely enjoy God's peace. An anxious Christian will always have difficulty finding the will of God. Why?

Because anxiety makes it so difficult to read the road signs in the light of God's Word.

Analytical by nature, Melancholies can dissect every aspect of a decision more thoroughly than anyone else. Even when confronted with a worthy goal, they'll occupy themselves with examining not only every roadblock, difficulty, or potential problem they *may* encounter on the journey—but a number of others that will never appear. If Melancholies make an ordinary task impossible by anticipating difficulties, just imagine what they can do to a difficult problem.

A thirty-year-old nurse, engaged for two years to a Christian man she'd dated for five years, asked to see me. She'd read all my books and was familiar with my example of the two melancholy preachers who were uncertain about marrying the women whom they eventually joined in wedlock. (One couple had been engaged eight times, had sent out wedding invitations twice—and cancelled the wedding both times! The other minister, who had been an NFL middle linebacker, only broke his engagement five times!) This nurse, seven weeks away from her own wedding, wondered if she should call it off. "I just don't seem to have peace about it." She admitted that she and her husband-to-be could've been married four years earlier had she not been so fearful. We examined the various road signs and Scripture passages—all of which merged except one: peace of heart. When I asked if she ever felt peace about anything, she hesitantly admitted that she didn't.

Decision making for her fomented a period of doubt, debate, perplexity, uncertainty—and personal agony. After I pointed out her lifetime pattern of anxiety, we submitted the marriage to God and asked Him to reveal something special to her in the coming weeks if she was not to marry her fiancé. I urged her to memorize Philippians 4:6–7 and practice praying with thanksgiving instead of anxiety. She prayed: "Heavenly Father, I thank you that you can guide me into making the right decision and that You love me too much to allow me to make the wrong decision. Please give me faith for my fears." And He did. Today they are married.

Remember the story in chapter 1 about Tom, the youth pastor who couldn't decide whether or not to marry the camp counselor? Tom's indecision also was affected by his melancholy temperament. As Tom and I talked about his problem, we looked at the road signs. Every one matched up except peace—and he felt peace only as long as the wedding day was several months away. But as the day approached, Tom's peace would evaporate. The more Tom and I talked, the more I became convinced that his lack of peace was more a function of his melancholy temperament than a sign from God not to marry. Under these circumstances, I advised him to ignore the sign. I told him, "The next time you get the urge to marry her, don't send out invitations. Just take her to Yuma and marry her!"

I flew back to San Diego and forgot all about it. Six months later I received a postcard from Yuma, Arizona, with these words: WE DID IT! When I saw Tom several months later, he gave me a bear hug and affirmed, "I wish someone had told me to do that five years earlier."

Melancholies rarely rush into decisions. Instead they drag them out interminably, and nothing is worse on emotional stability than indecision. It is right and proper to examine the road map and the highway signs, but once you have found them properly lined up, accept that as God's leading and make the decision. Once it's made, God will warn you during the savoring period if you have erred. You can trust the peace of God, but you can't trust the anxiety of your human spirit.

Melancholies more than any other temperament type are driven to the Word of God and their knees in times of uncertainty or adversity, and that is a safe harbor for any temperament. Thus decision-making times become for them times of deep spiritual growth. Melancholies also are more likely to ask others for advice, which is extraordinarily helpful if they seek spiritually motivated and informed counselors.

The best advice I can give to Melancholies is to spend time daily in the Word, pray with thanksgiving, and ask God to strengthen their faith. They should practice looking to God rather than to the problems conjured up by an analytical and fear-prone mind. Granted, they should be realistic about potential problems, but they shouldn't let anxiety magnify them out of proportion. Remember the spies of Israel? They had "grasshopper vision." Spotting the giants of Canaan, they identified themselves as "grasshoppers in their sight." By contrast, Caleb and Joshua saw the giants but viewed them through the eyes of faith. Instead of grumbling or lamenting, they told the Israelites not to fear because the Lord was with them. Such confidence quickly reduces giants to a manageable size.

Melancholies are perfectionists by nature. If they can't answer all questions perfectly, they tend to become immobilized. They fail to understand that even in leading us to do His perfect will, God requires an element of faith. When the road signs and God's Word agree, they should step out in faith unless God leads in some special way. If they sincerely seek to do God's will, He will reveal it to them. Our Lord promised, "If anyone wants to do His will, he shall know concerning the doctrine, whether it is from God or whether I speak on My own authority" (John 7:17 NKJV). While this text relates to Christ's deity and sovereignty, it explains how God leads those who are really committed to doing His will.

Phlegmatics at Decision Time

The practical side of the quiet, gentle Phlegmatic tends to simplify the decision process of life. But once they know God's will, they often lack the faith to step out and do it. They may be blessed with an objectivity about others' problems and be able to render good advice to friends, but an obsessive self-protection and hesitancy to get involved makes them vacillate and worry about consequences almost as much as the Melancholies do. When Phlegmatics examine what's involved and how God's purposes will affect them, they lose their objectivity.

It always pains me to remind Phlegmatics that they tend to be selfish people—selfish about giving their love, themselves, their possessions, and their service. Thus every decision to take action is shrouded in the complexity of resistance. Because they tend to be stubborn, the more someone tries to push them, the more they resist. Consequently, they may reject the advice of well-meaning friends.

Phlegmatics will never openly rebel at God's will, but they will refuse to act on it. Unless they're deeply surrendered to doing His will—no matter what the cost—they will decline a positive response more diplomatically than any other temperament.

Phlegmatics' preoccupation with self-protection hinders them from making many decisions. As pastor of a church for many years, I found that a public display of spiritual decisions was difficult for Phlegmatics. Many attended our church for a long time and were confident it was the place God wanted the family to attend, but only at the insistence of other family members would they take the public steps necessary to become a member.

Phlegmatics need to examine their motives whenever making a decision. If the road signs match up, yet they hesitate, they need to ask, "Am I resisting because I'm afraid of the consequences, or am I protecting myself rather than serving God?" They need to throw off the shell of self-protection, abandon themselves to the will of God, and pray, "Lord, what do you want me to do?" He hasn't saved any of us to be potted plants but tools in His hand for reaching others.

• • •

For free information on how you can take a complete temperament test that will give positive suggestions for your temperament weaknesses, write

LaHaye Temperament Analysis
370 L'Enfant Promenade, S.W., Suite 801
Washington, D.C. 20024

(Also, see the information and the attached coupon at the back of this book.)

13

What to Do
When You "Blow It"

Christians are not perfect. Even the best of us sin. It's idealistic and unrealistic to expect life to be otherwise, particularly in our bewildering, disordered culture. And I'm not simply alluding to the complexity of life in this high-tech, information age that has made decision making more complicated than it was throughout most of the world's history. I also include the topsy-turvy public policy that has turned morality on its head until almost everything that was considered evil just one generation ago is considered acceptable today. Our society approves of fornication, adultery, and perversion—as long as one is careful not to suffer the consequences by getting pregnant or contracting AIDS. The immorality of murder was made legal by the seven members of the Supreme Court so that abortion becomes an option for those who sin. We are spending literally billions of dollars trying to help people escape the consequences of their sin.

But even before God's moral code was inverted by public policy, becoming a Christian didn't guarantee a perfect life or perfect decisions. It's so rare to find anyone who hasn't sinned after becoming a Christian. Two people in the Old Testament who come to mind are Daniel and possibly Noah. Everyone else in the Bible, from Adam to the disciple John, "blew it" at some point in his or her life.

So don't be surprised if you wake up one day to discover that your good intentions have turned to improper thoughts and actions. The bad news is that turning from the path of God's will may prove very costly, for Scripture declares, "The way of transgressors is hard" (Prov. 13:15 KJV). The good news is that God isn't finished with you yet. He still has a plan for your life and has even provided means whereby you can find the "on ramp" to the avenue of His perfect will.

People Who Blew It

Many of God's greatest servants blundered miserably at some point, yet God forgave and restored them. But even though they repented of their sin, were forgiven, and experienced renewal, their disobedience cost them dearly.

We've already noted that Abraham sinned by running down into Egypt when faced with the impending famine in the land God promised him. While in Egypt, he lied about his wife and tried to palm her off as his sister. Yet after he repented, God used him to father many nations.

David, the second king of Israel, is a notorious example of failure because his moral collapse was so complete. But after much suffering and soul-wrenching guilt, David repented and returned to God, who used him to lead the nation for many years.

The prophet Jonah rebelled at God's specific call to go to Nineveh and preach a message of judgment to the people. Instead, Jonah's hatred toward those people overruled his spirit of obedience, and he deliberately boarded the ship to Tarshish. As a result, God sent judgment in the form of a storm. Jonah was thrown overboard, swallowed by a great fish, and eventually thrown up onto the land. At this point he obeyed God, boldly proclaimed his message to the Ninevites, and fomented a revival that turned the entire city to God.

The New Testament is full of similar stories: Peter, who denied his Lord; Paul, who stubbornly determined to go up to Jerusalem; John Mark, who abandoned Paul and Barnabas on the first missionary journey; and many others.

Both the biblical record and church history verify that God is "the God of the second chance." That doesn't mean that He looks lightly on sin. But unless we commit "the sin unto death" (1 John 5:16 KJV), which seems to represent long-term rebellion and open sin against God's will, we can be forgiven and restored. If you blow it with a major decision, you probably won't be able to complete God's perfect will for your life. But as I've already pointed out, you still can do His acceptable or good will.

A very able minister committed adultery. After his deed was discovered, he resigned the ministry of the local church. Like David of old, he sincerely repented of his sin. While God has used him in several effective areas, he has not as yet (after five years) been able to find a church that will call him as their pastor—even though he's an excellent preacher. Only God knows whether or not he'll ever pastor a church again.

Unfortunately, there are many such tragedies today, and I'm not aware of any that have been restored to God's perfect will. And while that doubtless causes people great pain and frustration, if they genuinely repent, God picks up the pieces of their lives and continues to use them, but in a different capacity.

Disobedience and Rebellion

Choosing to follow our own self-will instead of following God's will is rebellious and disobedient. And God doesn't look lightly on these sins. The Bible tells us that "rebellion is as the sin of witchcraft" (1 Sam. 15:23a NKJV). That is a serious charge; witchcraft in the Old Testament was a capital offense.

Willful rebellion is evident in some Christians today. A woman in one of my Bible classes refused to return to my class because she took issue with my teaching. When she heard me affirm that obedience to the will of God is the key to happiness and that disobedience is the key to misery, she rebelled. Why? Because she was a member of the self-indulgent generation who expect a loving, benevolent God to overlook the sins of His children and excuse their willful behavior. It's just a matter of time before such a person either destroys or limits her life as a tool in God's hand—unless she repents.

Consequences of Disobeying God's Will

God doesn't overlook our disobedience of His will. Instead, He chastens His children with judgment—because He loves us. The New Testament tells us, "Now no chastening seems to be joyful for the present, but grievous; nevertheless, afterward it yields the peaceable fruit of righteousness to those who have been trained by it. Therefore . . . make straight paths for your feet, . . . pursue peace with all men, and holiness, without which no one will see the Lord" (Heb. 12:11–14 NKJV). If we are truly Christians, God chastens us when we get out of His will.

God chastens us not only through His judgment but also through the natural consequences of our sin. When we disobey, we have to live with the natural consequences of our actions. For example, Becky, the young girl mentioned in chapter 1, was suffering the devastating consequences of becoming pregnant before she was married. Dick, the unfaithful husband mentioned in chapter 1, lived with the consequences of his adultery even after he had repented. He lived in fear, dreading the possibility that his wife would find out about his affair. He was certain that his "partner in crime" would divulge their secret and the story would get back to his wife. This fear contributed to his first bout with male impotence—a high price to pay for sin. Two different men I've counseled claimed that their first acts of infidelity resulted in herpes, an incurable venereal disease. Both escaped God's judgment through repentance, but they didn't elude the harmful physical effect and the consequences of such a disease in their marital relationship.

In his excellent little book, *Knowing the Will of God & Doing It,* Dr. Grant Howard itemizes some of the natural consequences of disobeying God.

> When we don't eat the right foods or get the proper rest and exercise, we have physical problems. Drinking and drugs can affect us physically, mentally, and emotionally, even to the point of addiction. When we keep to ourselves things that ought

to be shared with others, we suffer the emotional problems that go with suppression. Seldom do we suffer alone. Our sin has secondhand consequences in the lives of others. Lost jobs, broken homes, ruptured relationships, automobile accidents, and other misfortunes affect many others besides ourselves. God has built into His world cause-and-effect relationships—natural consequences that will inevitably take place. When we violate these natural laws or seek to outwit them, we pay the consequences. The Word does not give us much revelation about the natural effects of bad behavior; it majors on what *is* bad behavior. But experience tells us much about it, and we have seen from our study of common sense that God expects us to learn from our experience.

There are *feelings of guilt*, which are unpleasant. Sometimes these feelings are unnecessary. If they are produced by a nonbiblical legalism or a failure to realize that one is righteous (not guilty) in Christ, then the person is doing battle with unnecessary feelings. But if the believer has chosen consciously and willfully to violate truth that he understands, then he will feel bad. If he doesn't, he ought to, as James says, "Be miserable and mourn and weep; let your laughter be turned into mourning, and your joy to gloom" (James 4:9). This is the constructive sorrow that results in repentance. Paul speaks of it in 2 Corinthians 7:9, 10.

We have seen from the experience of David in Psalm 32 that guilt feelings can be extremely unpleasant. The United States Internal Revenue Service can attest to the same fact, since that office receives thousands of dollars every year from citizens who cheated on their income tax returns in the past and cannot live with their guilt feelings any longer.

For the Christian it is the Word of God applied by the Spirit of God that is making him aware of what is wrong in his life. Ephesians 6:17 indicates that the sword of the Spirit is the Word of God, and 2 Timothy 3:16 informs us that the Word is profitable for both reproof and correction. Thus, when we have violated God's Word, He makes us aware of this fact, and the awareness carries with it the unpleasant consequences of guilt feelings. The only way to deal with these adequately is by confession—to God and man.*

The Importance of Time in Disobedience

When we turn from the path of God's will, we need to be restored. And the key to being restored to God's perfect will is *time*. That is, if you allow too much time to elapse between sin and repentance, you can so mar your life that you may never again be able to do God's perfect will. Choices and decisions close in on us every day. Therefore, the longer we spend in rebellion to God's will, the more bad decisions we will make, which in turn increases the difficulty of being restored in time to fulfill His perfect will.

In addition, during the early days of sin, our conscience is more easily pricked, and we become acutely aware of being out of fellowship with God. As time goes on, however, the conscience becomes calloused, and we turn a deaf ear to the call of the Spirit. Some Christians even try to justify their sin in spite of clear biblical teaching. They didn't begin that way, but gradually the call of God's Holy Spirit fades. When God deems it sufficient time, He invokes His hand of

*J. Grant Howard, "Counsel and the Will of God," *Knowing God's Will and Doing It!* (Grand Rapids: Zondervan, 1976), 94–95.

judgment. Eventually, we hear His voice or suffer His chastening.

For that reason, I urge you to use these steps of restoration as soon as you discover that you are violating His will.

Seven Steps to Restoration

Step 1: Face Your Disobedience as a Sin

Unwillingness to face sin is one of the oldest sins. When God confronted our father Adam with his disobedience in the Garden of Eden, Adam protested that the woman God had given him caused him to sin (Gen. 3:12). Rather than face his sin and find restoration, Adam blamed Eve and justified himself.

Whatever the sin, I'm confident you are clever enough to contrive a shrewd excuse to justify it. After thirty years in the counseling room, I've heard almost every excuse possible. But self-vindication can never provide a remedy for sin. Until we are truly willing to say with the Prodigal Son, "I have sinned against heaven and in your sight, and am no longer worthy to be called your son" (Luke 15:21 NKJV), we are incapable of change. Refusing to blame his father, his friends, or God, the son took full responsibility for his actions. That is true repentance—and the initial giant step toward restoration.

Step 2: Repent of Your Self-Will

The classic definition for repentance indicates it is "a godly sorrow for sin, which produces an inward turning in obedience to God." That was the experience of King David after his appalling sin, as described in many of his psalms: "Blessed is he whose transgression is forgiven, whose sin is covered. Blessed is the man to whom the LORD does not impute iniquity, and in whose spirit there is no guile. When I kept silent, my bones grew old through my groaning all the day long. For day and night Your hand was heavy upon me; my vitality was turned into the drought of summer" (Ps. 32:1–4 NKJV).

Obviously, David's guilt, shame, and remorse had brought him to such despair that "his vitality was gone." Disobedience to God and the guilt it produces will do that to a Christian. But such contrition is a sign that the child of God is repentant. In the midst of that misery, repentant Christians, no matter how far into sin they have gone or how long they have wallowed in it, can turn to their merciful Father and repent of self-will, which is what produced the sin originally. While it's good to confess our "sins," the real problem is the singular sin of self-will. When Christ holds the reins of our life, we do not' sin. He never leads us to sin. Therefore, we must repent of self-will, which will result in refraining from "sins."

Step 3: Confess All Known "Sins"

The New Testament tells us, "If we confess our sins, he is faithful and just and will forgive us our sins and purify us from all unrighteousness" (1 John 1:9). David parallels that promise in Psalm 32:5: "Then I acknowledged my sin to you and did not cover up my iniquity. I said, 'I will confess my transgressions to the LORD'—and you forgave the guilt of my sin."

God in His marvelous grace seems willing to keep on cleansing us from all sin—*if* we confess! That not only rids our conscience of guilt but also enables us to avoid some of the consequences of sin. After telling us to judge our own sin, the apostle Paul added, "For if we would judge ourselves, we would not be judged" (1 Cor. 11:31 NKJV). God seems to permit a time lapse between our sin and His judgment. If we will repent and confess in the name of His Son, we can gain forgiveness and be spared God's judgment. That doesn't mean we'll avoid the consequences of sin. As the story of Alison in chapter 1 illustrates, confessing her sin didn't remove the pregnancy that resulted from her affair with a married man. She still had to suffer the humiliation of telling her family and bearing an illegitimate child. And it cost the man his position of leadership in the church and the financial liability of fathering a child out of wedlock, which in turn necessitated that he tell his wife—and the consequences may be protracted almost beyond endurance. But because both repented and confessed their sin, they avoided any additional judgment of God.

Step 4: Re-surrender the Control of Your Life to God

Repentance and confession are not complete until we return in obedience to God. The Lord warned us not to be like "The horse or the mule ... which must be bridled ..." before they obey Him. He said, "I will instruct you and teach you in the way you should go; I will counsel you and watch over you" (Ps. 32:8–9). He then leaves it to us to surrender to His will. Any time we are not surrendered or yielded to His will we are disobedient to Him (Rom. 8:11–13; 12:1–2).

God has a will for your life, and the first step is always to surrender to it—even before you know what it is. You will demonstrate that surrender by pursuing His known will today. That becomes the key to discovering His will for tomorrow.

Step 5: Examine Your Daily Devotional Habits

We often slip outside the circle of God's will because we lack fellowship with Him. Accordingly, we must read, study, and memorize the Word on a regular basis—as David said, "that [we] might not sin against [God]" (Ps. 119:11).

Daily devotions, like eating, need not be prolonged to become effective. Sometimes you eat at a leisurely pace; at other times you grab a quick bite before running off to work. In either case, you ingest some nutritional value. Even a few minutes spent reading God's Word in the morning and just before going to bed can give you a message from God. Then you can talk with Him in prayer as you proceed to work or as you reflect on your day before falling asleep. Remember, you can't fellowship or walk with Him unless you are going His way. The apostle John explained that to have fellowship with Him, we must "walk in the light, as he is in the light" (1 John 1:7). If we walk in darkness (which is outside the will of God), we're kidding ourselves if we think we're walking with Him (1 John 1:6–7).

Daily devotions are essential if we want to walk with Christ down the path of life. And they act as a safeguard to help us find His will. As we saw in chapter 6, the Bible is our road map for living, leading us to the center of God's perfect will.

Step 6: Assess Your Circumstances in the Light of God's Road Signs

If you have been out of fellowship with God for some time, go back to chapter 7 and reacquaint yourself with the road signs. Memorize them and follow their direction carefully. Gradually you'll find yourself in His good will, His acceptable will, or His perfect will. This, of course, will be determined by how long you were out of His will, how much you disobeyed, what kind of decisions you made while out of his will, and the consequences of your sin. But God always holds out to us the possibility of at least doing His good will—unless, of course, a Christian's restoration occurs on his or her deathbed.

The most dramatic biblical story of restoration from sin appears in the life of Samson, one of the judges of Israel. When Samson walked in God's will, he was endowed with superhuman strength. But then he forfeited God's perfect will by abusing the gifts God gave him, breaking God's moral law, living in sin outside of wedlock with an unbeliever, and violating his covenant with God by having his hair cut. Very few believers have squandered more talent and opportunity than the disobedient Samson. His judgment is well known: he lost his power, was captured by the enemy, and was blinded by his oppressors. Yet even blind Samson repented and was given one last opportunity to serve God. In so doing, he destroyed more of God's enemies in his death than he had in his life (see Judges 14–16).

As long as you have life, God can use you. Admittedly, you may not be able to fulfill God's perfect will, but you can enjoy His forgiveness and make yourself available to His good will—whatever it is.

Consider John, the minister referred to in chapter 1, who jeopardized his ministry by committing adultery. When he and his wife came to me, they were trying to decide whether or not God wanted them to tell the church about the adultery. As it turned out, someone else had made that decision for them. The "other woman" had confided her sin in just one other person, her best friend. That was one person too many. Soon the whole congregation knew about the affair, and John was forced to resign in disgrace from his pastorship.

Because John genuinely repented of his sin, however, he was able to rededicate his life to God's service. Although the Lord never allowed him to become a senior pastor again, John began winning souls to Christ and today is an extremely effective minister of evangelism in a large church, teaching others how to share their faith. See Chart I for what John's life chart would look like.

Contrast John with the Bible teacher who committed the same sin and is still wallowing in self-pity over the way he ruined his life. While God has forgiven him, he has never forgiven himself and consequently enjoys no effective ministry today.

God wants to use your life—from wherever you are *today!*

Step 7: Thank God by Faith for His Anticipated Leading

Groveling in shame, guilt, and remorse after repenting is never God's will. One of Satan's techniques is to demotivate repentant Christians as a means of keeping them from serving God. True, you may run into roadblocks when you return to your church and find that you no longer qualify for service as a minister, deacon, Sunday school teacher, or leader. *But don't let that destroy your spirit.*

Remember, forgiveness can take place the moment you repent and confess your sin in the name of Jesus. Restoration to service, however, takes time. Some Christians get angry or disillusioned because they're not instantly restored to their former place of service or leadership. That's unreasonable. Even newborn Christians are not eligible for such service but must prove themselves, according to Scripture. If you have rebelled at God's will and have sinned, you've demonstrated yourself untrustworthy and must now *reapprove* yourself. That takes time! And it requires maintaining a good attitude.

The Re-surrendered Christian

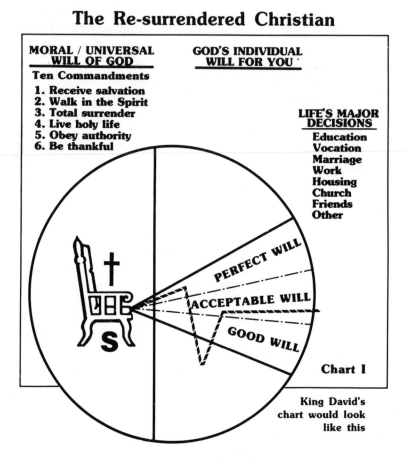

MORAL / UNIVERSAL WILL OF GOD

Ten Commandments
1. Receive salvation
2. Walk in the Spirit
3. Total surrender
4. Live holy life
5. Obey authority
6. Be thankful

GOD'S INDIVIDUAL WILL FOR YOU

LIFE'S MAJOR DECISIONS
Education
Vocation
Marriage
Work
Housing
Church
Friends
Other

PERFECT WILL
ACCEPTABLE WILL
GOOD WILL

S

Chart I

King David's chart would look like this

Don't mistakenly conclude that the good favor of people may be equated with the approval of God. If you were a church leader or an experienced Christian before getting out of God's will, don't expect to rush back into leadership as if nothing has happened. If you brought disrepute to the cause of Christ, it will take time to reestablish your eligibility for leadership and church approval. Many churches will institute a probationary period lasting a year or more before restoring a formerly mature Christian to positions of responsibility. The Bible gives no specific time schedule for reinstatement.

Believers who have abandoned the path of God's will primarily need spiritual approval from God. Forgiveness is instant, but now they must rebuild their flabby spiritual muscles through Bible study and daily walking in the Spirit—always keeping their eyes on the goal of serving Him. Remember this principle: the person who is "faithful over a few things" will be made "ruler over many things" (Matt. 25:21 NKJV). Start out small. Be humble. Be faithful at the outset where you are—your home, your neighborhood, your work. But above all, concentrate on leading others to Christ.

Everywhere you look, people need Jesus. As you trust God to enable you to win souls to Him, He will open other doors to you. One former Christian leader led several neighbors to Christ after his restoration, and inaugurated a Bible study in his home for them. It grew rapidly until it eventually became a church. Today he is pastoring that growing congregation. His sin, which was never hidden, is a thing of the past.

Wherever you are in this complex world, God wants to use you. Let Him do this by being faithful where you are, and gradually your doors of opportunity will open more fully. God has given you life, talent, salvation, His Word, His Holy Spirit, Bible knowledge, and opportunities. Forget those things that are in your past and press on in faithful, obedient service today and for the rest of your life—and you will hear Him say, "Well done, good and faithful servant. . . . Enter into the joy of your lord" (Matt. 25:21). You may ask, "What about my confessed sin?" Forget it! God has. His Word tells us that He remembers our sins against us *"no more"* (Heb. 10:17).

David, the Man After God's Own Heart

We've already noted that King David, during an eighteen-month period of his life, "blew it" about as badly as any human being could—lust, adultery, deception, misuse of authority, murder, etc. Yet after his chastening, repentance, judgment, remorse, and restoration, God used David to lead the nation for many years. Paul said of David, "After removing Saul, [God] made David their king. He testified concerning him: 'I have found David son of Jesse a man after my own heart; he will do everything I want him to do'" (Acts 13:22). Chart I gives a good graphic representation of King David's situation.

What about David's sin? It was forgiven! And so is yours, if you have repented and confessed it. Now spend the rest of your life serving God. This confused, empty-hearted world needs you.

▷ *You can be guaranteed a full, happy life only if it is one of service to Him.*

Someone has said, "You can spend your life any way you like—but you can only spend it once!" It is my prayer, now that you have read this book, that you will spend the rest of your life doing the perfect, or acceptable, or good will of God. Depending on which is still open to you, of one thing I am certain—when you get into heaven, you will not regret your choice.

LaHaye
Temperament
Analysis

- a test to identify your primary and secondary temperaments
- a description of your predominant characteristics
- information regarding your vocational aptitudes and possible vocations suited to you
- recommendations on improving your work habits
- a list of your spiritual gifts, in the order of their priority
- suggestions for where you can best serve in your church
- steps for overcoming your ten greatest weaknesses
- counsel on marital adjustment and parental leadership
- special advice to singles, divorcees, pastors, and the widowed

Your personal 13-to-16-page evaluation letter from Dr. Tim LaHaye will be permanently bound in a handsome vinyl leather portfolio.

... your opportunity
to know yourself
better!

$5.00 Discount Certificate
Off regular price of $24.95

_____
Name

_____
Address

_____
City

_____
State/Zip

Send this Discount
Certificate and your
Check for just $19.95
to:

Family Life Seminars
370 L'Enfant Promenade, S.W., Suite 801
Washington, D.C. 20024

Be sure to read these excellent books about temperaments by Tim LaHaye: